T4-ACM-816

THREE BIOGRAPHICAL ESSAYS

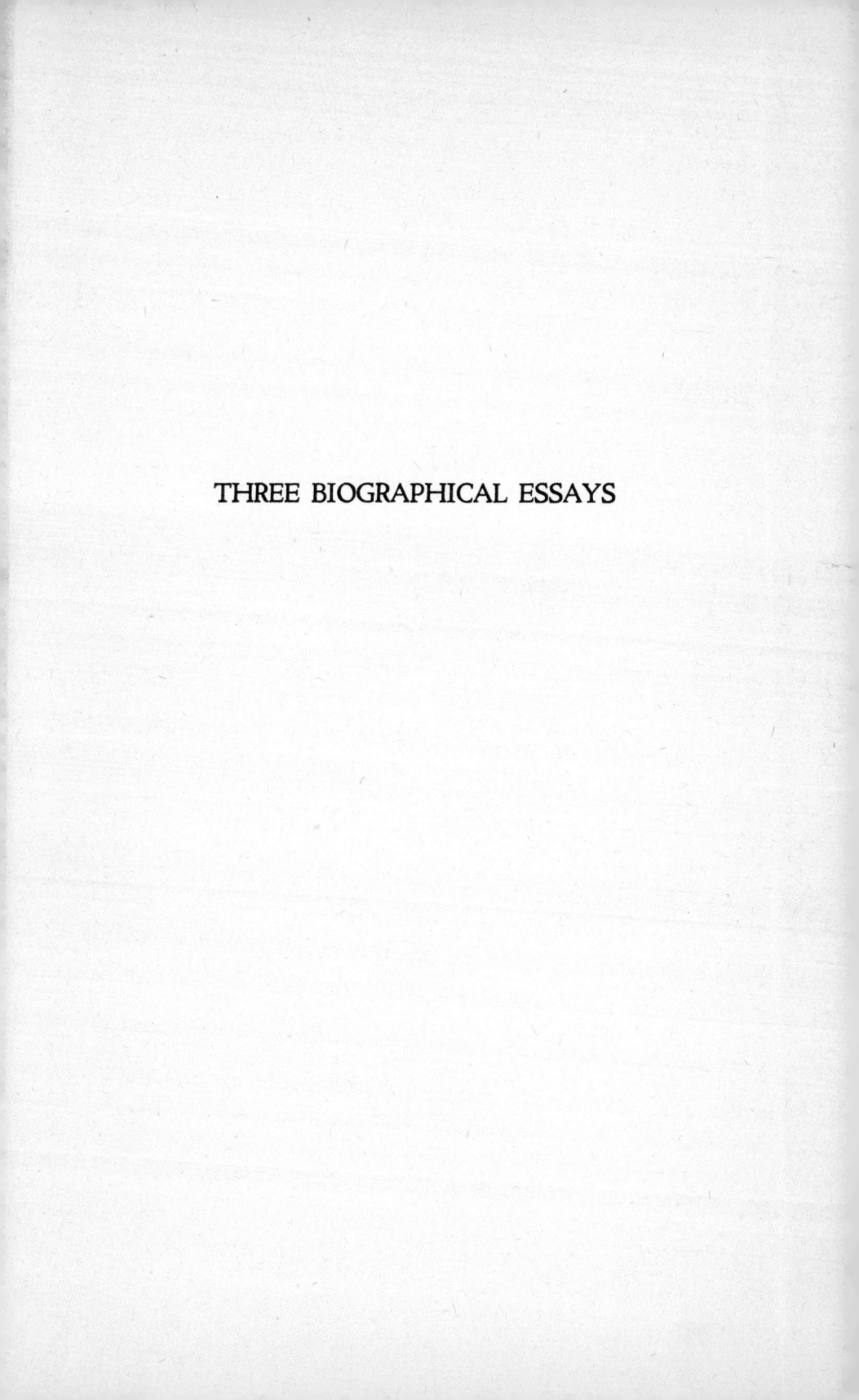

THREE ARCHBISHOPS
OF MILWAUKEE

Michael Heiss   (1818-1890)
Frederick Katzer   (1844-1903)
Sebastian Messmer (1847-1930)

by

THE REV. BENJAMIN J. BLIED, PH.D.

1955
MILWAUKEE, WISCONSIN

By the same Author:

Austrian Aid to American Catholics 1830-1860
Catholics and the Civil War
The Catholic Story of Wisconsin
Catholic Aspects of
    The War for Independence
    The War of 1812
    The War with Mexico
    The War with Spain

Nihil obstat:
    John A. Schulien, S.T.D., Censor librorum.
    Milwaukiae, die 24 Martii 1955.

Imprimatur:
    ✠Albertus G. Meyer, Archiepiscopus Milwaukiensis.
    Milwaukiae, die 25 Martii 1955.

Copyright 1955 by the Rev. Benjamin J. Blied

Printed in the United States of America

CONTENTS

	Page
PREFACE	7

ESSAY

I. MICHAEL HEISS	9
II. FREDERICK KATZER	46
III. SEBASTIAN MESSMER	82

PREFACE

After Pope Gregory XVI had been made aware of the administrative problems which the great western movement posed for the Church in the United States, he established the diocese of Milwaukee and appointed John M. Henni its first bishop. This was in 1843. Unaided as well as untrammeled by the pattern of any predecessor, this industrious Swiss immigrant developed the resources of his frontier see, and, being blessed with length of days, he saw it attain metropolitan rank in 1875. This first archbishop is fairly well remembered but the next three remain relatively unknown.

None the less they deserve notice. Their careers, dating from Heiss' arrival in Wisconsin as a young priest and extending down to Messmer's death at a patriarchal age, cover eighty-six years. For half a century these three held in unbroken succession the highest ecclesiastical office in Wisconsin. All three were south Germans: Heiss was a Bavarian, Katzer an Austrian, and Messmer a Swiss. Naturally the European backgrounds of these men influenced their conduct in the new world. Moreover, all three had strong convictions coupled with inflexible wills. Consequently, when they tackled the problems that were created by a new nation, a dominantly Protestant population, an unprecedented industrial development, and a policy of unrestricted immigration, they frequently set off controversies with their peers and their subjects.

Almost no literature exists concerning them, and few of their public documents and private papers escaped destruction. Therefore it seemed advisable to include in these essays numerous, lengthy quotations. Their quaint or awkward phraseology often points to the foreign origin of the author. Moreover, this work appears without a bibliography. Extensive footnotes, however, aim to take its place. Needless to say, these essays, which were published in much shorter form in magazines, are explorative rather than definitive.

The author wishes to thank Rev. Raymond Fetterer of the Salzmann Library without whose help these essays could not have been written. He thanks Rev. Thomas T. Mc Avoy, C. S. C., of Notre Dame University, the Benedictine Fathers at St. John's University, Collegeville, Minn., and the staff of the Central Verein for access to their libraries and archives. Lastly, he thanks the Rt. Rev. Msgr. Peter Leo Johnson and Rev. David Wilbur for giving the manuscript a critical reading.

I

MICHAEL HEISS

Karl Boeswald was the kind of student that didn't squander all his time at cards or in the gymnasium. Nor did he submerge himself in his textbooks so deeply as to be oblivious of contemporary events.

One day he read that thousands of Germans in America were without priests who spoke their language. Here was an outlet for his youthful vigor. He dashed off a letter to a young priest telling him of his decision.

"So Karl wants to go to America", mused the recipient.

"If you go, I'm going along", relayed Father Heiss.

"I'm going", came the answer, "I've made up my mind. Come along then."

But Boeswald was subject to military service. Friends in high places availed nothing. He simply could not leave Bavaria before he received subdeaconship. Heiss wavered but his bishop urged him to carry out his resolution despite the reluctance of his parents. These found it exceedingly hard to part with the youngest of their five children.

Michael had been born to Joseph Heiss and Gertrude Frei at Pfaldorf in the district of Kipfenberg, Bavaria, on April 12, 1818. That same day he was baptized Michael.[1] When he was two years old he was confirmed because the Bavarians feared that they might be without a bishop for a long time owing to the mounting tension between church and state. After attending the parish school young Michael went to the Latin school at Eichstaett. Later he transferred to the gymnasium in Neuburg, and then he matriculated at the Georgianum, the clerical seminary

---

[1] Michael outlived his brothers and sisters. His parents died a few months apart in 1856 or 1857.

in Munich. His life in this center of culture was much freer than that of a seminarian today and his studies, though more stimulating, were less thoroughly permeated by the spirit of the Church. So much so was this the case that he made his first retreat only after finishing theology. In 1840, on October 18, Bishop Reisach of Eichstaett ordained him a priest in a convent chapel at Nymphenburg, near Munich, where the bishop happened to be attending to official business.

Because he was too young for ordination he had acted as prefect in the new and thoroughly ecclesiastical seminary in Eichstaett. After his ordination his task was to care for several poor, rural parishes. Like every young priest just ordained, he went about his work with genuine apostolic zeal but he never felt that he had attained his ultimate goal in life. Some years back when Bishop Purcell of Cincinnati visited the Georgianum he felt an urge to go with him to America. All along he kept thinking about the missions. Lovable Dr. Ernst of the Eichstaett seminary encouraged him to translate his dream into reality, and, since his bishop concurred, the next move was to apply for his traveling expenses at the office of the Ludwig Mission Society in Munich. With $300 tucked away in his pocket, he went via Strasbourg to Paris where he met Father William Schonat, a priest from Munich bound for Ohio. After dallying several days in the quaint *rues* around St. Sulpice they continued their journey going through Normandy via Rouen to Havre. Here a three master waited to take them across the ocean. They docked in New Orleans on December 16, 1842. Both then proceeded up the Mississippi and the Ohio to Louisville. After eight days of phlegmatic river travel Heiss was in a position to make the observation that the Ohio valley was far more picturesque than the Mississippi.

A few months later Boeswald followed Heiss to Kentucky. Neither of them had a personal predilection for this state. They came here because Reisach, their bishop, suggested it. He, in turn, had been influenced by Bishop Flaget[2] of Louisville who had pleaded for German priests. Though born in the diocese of Eichstaett, as prefect of studies at the Propaganda College in Rome, Reisach became acquainted with many American bishops. His interest in the missions was further intensified by the Ludwig Mission Society which was the Bavarian counterpart to the Leopoldine Society of Austria.[3] As soon as Heiss arrived, Flaget inquired about Reisach. This old patriarch of Kentucky, who had lost his teeth and much of his hearing, kept repeating again and again to Heiss how glad he was that he had come. Heiss rested only a few days in Louisville, but he did have time enough to learn how lax the German Catholics had become. Duly disillusioned, the new missionary left by boat for Covington to take charge of a church which Father Kuhr, one of Reisach's *ordinati,* had recently established. Here, besides serving the city, he made excursions into the surrounding country familiarizing himself with the people and developing the much needed skills of an equestrian.

Within a month after his arrival in the United States, Heiss either perceived the significance of the public school system or, what is more likely, confirmed antecedent opinions. He wrote to Dr. Ernst early in 1843: Schools "are supported by the state, but follow the principle not to teach any religion, to tell the children nothing about Christ, but to teach them a kind of pagan morality. These schools are more and more patronized by our infidels, and will, humanly speaking, be one of the chief causes of the total downfall of religion in the United States . . . . No child of German parents frequents the public schools; for it is better to have their education neglected than to have their souls

---

[2]Flaget, a refugee from the French Revolution, was the first bishop of Bardstown. When founded in 1808 this diocese embraced the entire west. He was closely connected with the French Society for the Propagation of the Faith. Starting in 1835 he spent several years in Europe lecturing on the American missions. He died in 1850.

[3]The Ludwig Mission Society was organized in 1838 but did not begin to function until the next year.

ruined."[4] And it was not long before he deflated reports of how the Church was flourishing. "Growth", said he, "is mainly due to immigration, and the few conversions are offset by the apostasy of many Catholics, particularly among our fellow Germans."[5]

Unlike Boeswald[6] who remained in Kentucky down to the time of his premature death in 1855, Heiss spent less than a year at Covington when he decided that little remained to be done in Kentucky. There were only two German parishes: one in Louisville and another in Covington. The likelihood of growth was slight because Germans did not migrate to that state "owing to the Negro slaves". So he asked the bishop for permission to leave. After a short delay it was granted but in such words that Heiss felt deeply hurt. Tears flowed when Boeswald relayed the bishop's comments. Heiss himself said that if he had not known a bishop it would have been hard for him to find another diocese.[7]

What to do? Having lived right across the river from Cincinnati, he had often visited in Ohio. Now he vacillated between joining Cincinnati and going to the new diocese of Milwaukee

---

[4] Heiss to Ernst, Feb. 1, 1843, *Salesianum*, April, 1914, pp. 14-5. At the time Kuhr was in Europe on a begging trip. Heiss asked that he be allowed to solicit gifts in case he came to Eichstaett.

[5] Heiss to Ernst, Jan. 8, 1844, *Salesianum*, July, 1914, p. 19. He also said: "The condition of a bishop in America is, as far as I can judge, so delicate that even with the best intention he cannot satisfy all the different nationalities."

[6] Boeswald was born on Feb. 27, 1820, in Wenden, Bavaria. After offering his first Mass in Covington he organized Corpus Christi parish at Newport, Ky. Next he organized St. Mary's on Eighth and Grayson St., Louisville. In 1852 he served as Bishop M. J. Spalding's theologian at the council of Baltimore. The following year he became chancellor of the diocese of Louisville. In 1855 a band of Know-nothings pelted Boeswald with stones while he was returning from a sick call. An abscess formed on his hip and caused his death on Nov. 2, 1855.

[7] Heiss to Kellermann, May 23, 1844, *Salesianum*, July, 1914, p. 22, reports favorably on Flaget's presence in the sanctuary at Henni's consecration. Heiss drove Flaget to Covington and recorded: "On this occasion I gained his favor to such a degree that he entirely forgave my leaving his diocese."

with Bishop Henni, formerly the pastor of Holy Trinity Church in Cincinnati. Finally he cast his lot with the latter. The frontier would be his destination. In the interim Heiss gave some missions in Ohio and the next spring he and Henni arrived in Milwaukee. The date was May 4, 1844.

Wisconsin did not become a state until 1848. Heiss, however, was rather comfortably located in Milwaukee charged with the care of the Germans, but, on the other hand, he also had to attend outlying missions. Right after his arrival he saddled his horse and made an exploratory trip in a northwesterly direction looking up Catholics near Goldendale and Hubertus.[8] Next he explored the environs of Burlington and Jefferson. And it was not long before he erected St. Mary's on Broadway Street which was one of the first brick structures to perpendicularize Milwaukee's skyline.

In one of his first letters from Milwaukee Heiss touched upon the school question. "Everywhere", wrote he, "we find public schools, but no religious instruction is permitted in them; and if our Catholic children are to be instructed in the catechism, which is more necessary here than in Germany, the Catholics, besides paying for the public schools, have to support their own schools. This causes an average expense of four to five dollars a year per child. But not all of our Catholics are zealous enough to make these sacrifices; the more so, if they have to pay board for their children, in case they live at some distance from the school. No one can compel them if not their conscience, which has to be aroused again and again when they come to confession; and more than once I was obliged to refuse them absolution."[9]

Heiss did not limit his sphere of activity to Wisconsin. He made a begging tour through Ohio on behalf of St. Mary's, and in 1849 he attended a provincial council of Baltimore as Bishop

---

[8] Heiss to the editor of the *Wahrheitsfreund*, June 27, 1844. He dates his first journey May 27, *Salesianum*, Oct., 1938, p. 182. He reviewed this trip in a letter to the Ludwig Mission Society on Aug. 30, 1861, *Salesianum*, Oct., 1945, p. 173.

[9] Heiss to Kellermann, May 23, 1844, *Salesianum*, July, 1914, p. 27.

Henni's theologian. The following year, feeling the need of a long rest, he went to Bavaria to convalesce in the congenial atmosphere of his home land. His work in the new world had gradually sapped his strength and late in 1845 he suffered a serious attack of typhoid and liver trouble.

While in Europe he acted as agent for the diocese and in 1851 he accepted the rather gifted Dr. F. X. Paulhuber for incardination. Unfortunately, his career in Wisconsin proved to be both stormy and brief.[10] Then, too, the Ludwig Mission Society found Heiss a storehouse of information and its officers thought it advisable to keep him in Munich as an official intermediary to deal with the American hierarchy. However, while Heiss rested and relaxed in Europe, tragedy struck Milwaukee. Cholera whisked away Fathers Keppeler and Steiger,[11] two Bavarian immigrants to Wisconsin, who had accompanied a small group of Franciscan sisters and brothers to St. Francis in 1849.

Deeply smitten by this double loss Bishop Henni became anxious for Heiss to return. Upon his arrival in 1852 the bishop sent him to St. Francis as spiritual director of the diminutive convent. At the same time he charged him with organizing a seminary. Heiss soon discovered that the convent did not function smoothly so he peremptorily discharged three members[12] and compiled a rule outlining the sisters' program in detail from their rising at 4:15 a. m. to their retiring at 9:00 p. m. In the course of his long sick leave he had served as convent chaplain at Ditramzell. This assignment may have been providential

---

[10]Paulhuber had been stationed in Ingolstadt and was first attracted to America by Henni. He arrived on June 2, 1851, served as pastor in Germantown and of St. Mary's in Milwaukee and supervised the construction of the seminary. In 1855 he went to Buffalo with a view to settling there but came back to Milwaukee. The following year he returned to Europe.

[11]Mileta Ludwig, *A Chapter of Franciscan History The Sisters of the Third Order of St. Francis of Perpetual Adoration 1849-1949* (New York, 1949), p. 395; Eunice Hanousek, *A New Assisi The First Hundred Years of the Sisters of St. Francis of Assisi, Milwaukee, Wisconsin, 1849-1949* (Milwaukee, 1948), pp. 22-24.

[12]Heiss to Kleiner, July 6, 1853, *Salesianum*, Jan., 1915, p. 26.

because it fitted him somewhat for his new kind of work. Though the seminary was only a dream, he incorporated institutional work in the sisters' routine. When the seminary finally became a reality in 1856, the bishop made Heiss rector, an office with prestige but without salary. Enthusiastic Father Salzmann, who had won the laurels of the doctorate in Austria, had the more disagreeable task of paying the endless bills. Mr. Bernard Durward, the third member of the original staff, taught English under a rector who, besides being somewhat anti-social, saw little merit in the language of Dryden and Shakespeare.

The sisters continued to claim some of Heiss' time until 1858 when he delegated Father Batz,[13] a Bavarian accession to the faculty, to take charge of the convent. This required considerable tact because the affairs of the convent were inextricably intertwined with those of the seminary. The latter held the title to the land of both establishments, the sisters worked in the seminary without a fixed salary, and Salzmann opposed their staffing schools or inducting more candidates than the seminary and St. Aemilian's Orphanage could support. Moreover, the sisters from Germany were willing to do more work than the recruits from the United States yet their foreign style of cooking did not satisfy American tastes. Batz, instead of attacking these problems, merely crystallized the discontent. Ruggedly or rancorously assailing their mode of life as not at all conventual, he stigmatized them as maids. If their routine did not lead to sanctity they might just as well leave. So in 1860 the remaining founders admitted defeat and departed with heavy hearts. Father Batz left the faculty immediately but Heiss could not undo what had happened. The secessionists hoped to be admitted to a convent in Germany, but,

---

[13]Batz, born in 1826, grew up two miles from Heiss' home. He studied at Eichstaett, Munich, and Wuerzburg. He came to America and was ordained here in 1858. After leaving the seminary as professor he served St. Mary's as pastor for twenty years. In 1879 Henni made him vicar general, in 1882 he was made monsignor. He died on May 26, 1901. Ireland and Keane in their rebuttal of Abbelen's *Relatio* listed Batz among those who believed that the English language deserved preference as the language of the land.

failing that, they became lifelong wards of Father Batz after his appointment to St. Mary's Church in Milwaukee.[14]

The eleven who stayed at St. Francis discharged their domestic duties at the seminary. Heiss appreciated that they had filled the breach and he reciprocated with some concessions. He authorized improvements in the convent property and consented to making the motherhouse less dependent upon the seminary. This meant picking a new location. First he thought of Roxbury, made famous by Father Inama, but eventually he chose Jefferson for the new convent. More than that, when the bishop allowed the sisters to teach school — to the dismay of Salzmann — Heiss helped to qualify them intellectually for the classroom. The community made some progress but the Jefferson venture did not prove to be an ideal solution to its problems.[15]

Obviously Heiss' first obligation was not taking care of the convent but of the seminary. Considering that he attended the University of Munich in the creative era of German Romanticism, it is no wonder that he had a taste for scholarship. He had studied under world renowned scholars such as Doellinger and Moehler and late in life he expressed his permanent indebtedness to two great books: the latter's *Symbolik* and Hurter's *Life of Innocent III*. Their example inspired him to compile a canonical treatise in Latin on matrimony which was published in Munich in 1861. This book, whose contents are extensive, developed somewhat in laboratory fashion as it was Heiss who handled the matrimonial cases that arose in the diocese. Because he attacked widespread abuses the author thought it would be hard to get an *imprimatur* for his work whereas his admirers feared it would block his way to the episcopate. Two years later a Milwaukee press printed a disquisition entitled *The Four Gospels Examined and Vindicated on Catholic Principles*. Besides these he compiled a German life

---

[14]One of them, Mother Aemiliana, outlived Batz. She died in 1904 as a guest of the La Crosse sisters. Ludwig, *op. cit.*, pp. 398-402.

[15]Heiss gave a retreat in 1861 to the Dominican Sisters from Regensburg who had settled in Green Bay. Heiss to the Ludwig Mission Society, Aug. 30, 1861, *Salesianum*, Jan., 1948, pp. 21-23.

of St. Peter Damian which never appeared in print.[16] Though his plans to write in the field of philosophy did not materialize, he did write some detailed memoirs of his youth which the German weekly, *Columbia,* reprinted in booklet form.

The record of Heiss' writings can easily be traced, but his work on the rostrum is elusive. First of all, he did not like teaching.[17] Second, he could never forget Bavaria. While teaching he dreamed of becoming confessor to the nuns at Beuerberg. Late in 1862 Father Mueller of Munich advised Bishop Henni that the position was open, adding quite correctly that Heiss would always be homesick.[18] If he wanted to return, now was the time. Nothing happened.

By then Heiss had witnessed significant political developments. Immediately after he came to Milwaukee the war with Mexico unleashed the stereotyped gossip about Catholic loyalty in view of the fact that all Mexicans were at least nominal Catholics. Next he saw the mushroom growth of the Know-nothing party which put Catholics in Buchanan's column in 1856, and when the seminary was just four years old the Republicans elected Abraham Lincoln. Forthwith seven states seceded. Four more followed. That meant war.

In 1862 Heiss commented: "The principles of right have been so much confused by false theories that both parties claim to be perfectly right. The south is in a bad plight just now, but there is no sign of compromise. It seems that they will rather perish than surrender."[19] The next year he wrote: "No one wants to hear of peace and those who counsel it are considered as traitors . . . . . Slavery is certainly a great evil, but if it is

---

[16]Heiss to Kleiner, June 14, 1858, *Salesianum,* July, 1915, p. 19, describes his life of St. Peter Damian as almost finished. On July 16, 1879, *Salesianum,* Jan., 1918, p. 32, he says he is still working on it. Same comment Jan. 1, 1881, *Salesianum,* April, 1918, p. 24.

[17]Heiss to Kleiner, May 4, 1847, *Salesianum,* Oct., 1914, p. 22; June 10, 1860, *Salesianum,* Oct., 1915, p. 23.

[18]Mueller to Henni, Dec. 5, 1862, *Salesianum,* July, 1948, p. 108.

[19]Heiss to Kleiner, June 21, 1862, *Salesianum,* Jan., 1916, p. 12.

suddenly abolished the south is ruined and the lot of the slaves is made worse rather than better . . . . . Do not believe that the friends of the Negroes, who are the cause of this war, are actuated by motives of charity. They only wished to get into power, to enrich themselves by the war, and to get possession of the rich products of the south . . . . . The constitution of the country has become a dead letter; the president has absolute power. The Catholics take a determined stand for the constitution but they do not stand for a government that wants to tyrannize everything without a constitution."[20] Heiss thought most Catholics wanted the war to end by compromise but expressing such thoughts was dangerous. Should a military despotism evolve, retribution would be swift and severe.

Analyzing political developments in the quiet of his study was one thing; running the seminary was another. Prices skyrocketed, the draft ensnared the professors, who were not exempt even if they were priests, and the students fled from the classrooms. In 1864 sixty disappeared in two days with the result that summer vacation started a month ahead of schedule. That year Heiss wrote to Europe: "The Union is in pieces and it seems that liberty will be exchanged for tyranny. The war is still raging; the southerners fight for their cause like lions and in the north the ruling faction has enough power to rush daily new victims into death."[21]

Like most German Catholics in the hinterland, Heiss probably voted the Democrat ticket and subscribed to P. V. Deuster's *Seebote*. This appeared in Milwaukee and regularly flayed the administration. Bishop Henni, though reticent, flew the flag from his cathedral and encouraged enlisting. Salzmann, however, deprecated Lincoln and found kind things to say about his fellow countryman, Maximilian of Mexico.[22]

---

[20]Heiss to Kleiner, July 4, 1863, *Salesianum*, April, 1916, p. 20.

[21]Heiss to Kleiner, July 4, 1864, *Salesianum*, April, 1916, p. 21.

[22]Salzmann to Ludwig Mission Society, July 31, 1867, *Salesianum*, April, 1947, p. 68, records his offering a solemn high Mass for the emperor. A crown stood on the catafalque.

Since Heiss came from Bavaria and Salzmann from Austria, their views on European developments differed. In 1859 when Napoleon III conquered Francis Joseph, Heiss confided to a correspondent: "Sometimes we have hot debates. Dr. Salzmann, being an Austrian, sides with Austria as a matter of course, while two other professors are just as strongly on the side of Napoleon III. I am neutral. My view of the question is this: This time Austria is in the right and is unjustly attacked but the Austrian government has by its Josephism done great harm and deserves great punishment for it. I hope you will have more patience with my views than my very good friend, Dr. Salzmann."[23] Apparently Heiss failed to stay neutral. In 1861 he confirmed all suspicions of domestic hostilities by assuring his addressee, Father Kleiner, that he was on good terms with Salzmann but "he tells the truth to me and I to him if necessary."

Just when the Civil War ended, the diocese of Milwaukee under the inspiration of Salzmann prepared to establish the Catholic Normal School adjacent to the seminary. It never prospered but owing to the genius of John Singenberger it served as the national headquarters for reform in church music for half a century. At the same time Heiss and a coterie of friends launched an ecclesiastical review, the *Pastoral-Blatt*. This appeared monthly in St. Louis from 1866 down to the end of 1925. The priests of St. Louis agreed to provide the funds if the professors at St. Francis would furnish the articles. In addition to sponsoring this venture in journalism, Heiss wrote for the Cincinnati *Wahrheitsfreund* under the pen name of *Caecus Videns*.

Precisely when the *Pastoral-Blatt* made its debut Heiss theorized about organizing the Clerical Society of the Immaculate Virgin Mary. Believing that American bishops were hesitant about enforcing stricter discipline and realizing the inadequacy of the routine retreats to reform the clergy, he proposed to bring priests together in frequent, intimate contacts so that they would inspire each other to fulfil their functions meticulously. The

---

[23] Heiss to Kleiner, July 21, 1859, *Salesianum*, Oct., 1915, p. 20.

common life with male instead of female housekeepers was one of its ideals, and the increased study of pastoral problems was another. The society would maintain a fund to help old and infirm priests, its members would shun the usual recreations in taverns and parks, including family celebrations, and, by way of compensation, all members would receive hospitality from fellow priests during life, and after death each member would receive three Masses from each of his colleagues. Bishop Henni approved the statutes and twenty-five priests volunteered to join but the project died at birth.[24]

None the less it shows how thoroughly the idea of the religious life had saturated Heiss. It further illustrates the inspiration which he drew from his home land, for it was the Venerable Bartholomew Holzhauser, a native of Bavaria, who propagated this idea which is said to have been endorsed by the Blessed Virgin herself in an apparition to Holzhauser at Ingolstadt. Despite the failure of this project and the limited success of the others, collectively they served to make Heiss' name well known far beyond the confines of the seminary and the diocese.

In July of 1866 Archbishop Spalding asked Heiss to come to Baltimore to prepare matters of canon law for the second plenary council. The choice was prudent because he had been in this country over twenty years, he had attended the council of 1849, and he headed an institution which was commanding increasing respect. Heiss accepted the invitation to the preliminaries and in autumn he attended the council with Bishop Henni, but on both occasions he took sick. Among the deliberations of the council was the need of additional dioceses. Two of the nine new sees were created in Wisconsin: one at La Crosse and another at Green Bay. Heiss was nominated for the former. Since this

---

[24]Heiss to Kleiner, June 22, 1867, *Salesianum*, July, 1916, p. 22, says Henni was cool to the project. Heiss to Kleiner, June 25, 1868, *Salesianum*, Oct., 1916, p. 2, says Henni was pleased with it. Peter Leo Johnson, "Bartholomites in Wisconsin", *Salesianum*, Jan., 1950, pp. 9-15. Salzmann to Ludwig Mission Society, Oct. 3, 1864, *Salesianum*, Jan., 1947, p. 22, speaks of Wapelhorst's coming to the seminary in connection with the project.

was generally known, he confided to his friends that if Rome rejected him he could hardly continue as rector.[25]

Before being consecrated this devotee of Holzhauser resolved to reform the north. In June of 1868 he wrote: "In the city of La Crosse, my future place of residence, there is only one priest and unfortunately one whom I do not like to see there, and, as he knows my sentiments, nothing is done in preparation for my coming. There is not even a priest's house there which would be large enough for two. And so I will probably have to rent a house when I come there. I expect to find similar conditions in at least seven other places where there are priests who know or suspect that I do not like to keep them. They remain only because they think that I need them owing to the scarcity of priests, but I am resolved to send those priests whom I cannot trust back to the diocese of Milwaukee where they belong even if some parishes should be without priests for some time."[26]

The months rolled by and on September 6, 1868, Bishop Henni laid his wrinkled hands upon the bushy head of his co-laborer to make him a peer unto the Apostles and unto himself. Assisting him were Bishops Lefevere of Detroit and Grace of St. Paul. Three weeks later the new bishop bade farewell to the seminary and on September 29, his patronal feast, he took possession of his throne in La Crosse.

While the city was congratulating itself on becoming the seat of a bishop, Heiss deflated any incipient civic pride by disclosing that the diocese had been projected thirteen and again nine years ago.[27] No one wanted it. At the time of his coming the region that constituted his diocese was destitute. It numbered less than a score of priests and these served 30,000 Catholics of seven nationalities scattered over an area the size of Bavaria.

---

[25] Heiss to Kleiner, June 22, 1867, *Salesianum*, July, 1916, p. 20.

[26] Heiss to Kleiner, June 22, 1868, *Salesianum*, Oct., 1916, p. 2. One of the victims was probably Father Smedding who edited the abortive *Romana* and criticized Heiss' scholarship. *Salesianum*, Jan., 1947, p. 15.

[27] Ludwig, *op. cit.*, p. 151.

Choosing a cathedral was problematic because La Crosse had only two churches. It was a case of exalting one and humbling the other. St. Mary's, the older of them, served the English and French speaking people; St. Joseph's, organized in 1863, served the Germans and Bohemians. For unrecorded reasons the bishop chose the latter with the inevitable result. The hard feelings were not limited to the parishioners nor were they quickly forgotten. Eighteen years later several eastern bishops still thought it worth while to accuse him of partisan motives in selecting his cathedral.[28] Although St. Joseph's had led an independent existence for five years before the creation of the diocese, the parish failed to flourish even after it attained the new dignity, and as late as the summer of 1869 the bishop wrote to Europe that his cathedral was only up to the windows.

Parenthetically it can be remarked that Heiss deferred becoming a citizen until he became a bishop. He applied for his papers on August 7, 1868, and received them on June 30, 1879.[29]

The new bishop had hardly become familiar with his see when the summons to the Vatican Council took him to Rome. On October 11, 1869, he and Henni left Milwaukee for New York where they boarded the *S. S. Lafayette*. Upon arrival Heiss was named to the committee on discipline. Unlike many prelates from Germany and in contrast to Bishops Henni of Milwaukee and Melcher of Green Bay, Heiss from the start favored defining papal infallibility.[30]

---

[28]*The German Question in the Church in the United States* by John Ireland and John Keane, dated Dec. 6, 1886. "In the city of La Crosse, the oldest and the strongest parish was the English parish. When Msgr. Heiss was made bishop of this place, he chose the German church for his cathedral, and even to this day, under his successor, we behold this strange phenomenon, that the official language of a Catholic bishop in an American city is a language foreign to the country. The same state of affairs exists at Green Bay, where a sermon in English is never heard in the cathedral on Sunday, the English Catholics being thus obliged to go to a neighboring city to receive religious instruction in the language of their country."

[29]Ludwig, *op. cit.*, p. 407.

[30]Raymond J. Clancy, "American Prelates in the Vatican Council", *Historical Records and Studies* of the U. S. Catholic Historical Society, vol. 28 (New York, 1937), pp. 40-2, 78.

Besides ruminating the problems of the universal church, he made inquiries about having the Franciscan sisters move their motherhouse from Jefferson to La Crosse. Finding no major canonical impediments, the transfer soon became an accomplished fact. If this irritated Bishop Henni,[31] Heiss stilled all scruples about fair play by recalling that he had practically founded the community, that the choice of Jefferson for the motherhouse had not been felicitous, and that Milwaukee was rich in sisterhoods in contrast to La Crosse.

After returning from the eternal city Heiss convened a synod at Prairie du Chien. He introduced the Franciscan Fathers of Teutopolis to care for northern Wisconsin;[32] he authorized the School Sisters of Notre Dame to conduct an academy at Prairie du Chien which in the twentieth century blossomed into Mt. Mary College in Milwaukee; the Christian Brothers located there as also the Benedictines; and the Jesuits established Sacred Heart College. He tried to get the Capuchins into his diocese but this failed just as did the attempt to keep the Benedictines at his cathedral.[33] Whether Heiss did any long range planning or just temporized from year to year is hard to say. Yet when he left La Crosse after an incumbency of twelve years, the number of priests had risen to 59, churches had increased from 47 to 101, and parish schools had increased from 2 to 24.

When Monsignor Roncetti brought the pallium to Bishop Henni in 1875 his old co-laborer in La Crosse must have been deeply impressed. Thirty-one years earlier Heiss had accompanied

---

[31] Ludwig and Hanousek advance different interpretations of Henni's reaction. The La Crosse group was larger than the group that remained at St. Francis.

[32] *The Friars Minor in the United States With a Brief History of the Orders in General* (Chicago, 1926), pp. 64-67. In 1878 Heiss entrusted St. Agnes church in Ashland to the Franciscans. He also gave them Bayfield, LaPointe, and the other Indian missions of his diocese. For some years they attended fifty Indian and White missions.

[33] Heiss to Kleiner, June 14, 1877, *Salesianum*, Oct., 1917, p. 42. Heiss to Woelfle, April 29, 1878, *Salesianum*, Jan., 1918, p. 27, says the Benedictines were to start a college in La Crosse. The abbot was timorous and nothing eventuated.

him to the outskirts of civilization when Wisconsin lacked even its first mile of railroad; he had played a major part in establishing his seminary; now he saw him receive well-deserved recognition. How much easier it would be to look to Milwaukee for leadership than to a metropolitan living down in St. Louis!

Milwaukee should have become an archdiocese when Heiss was consecrated for La Crosse. Heiss was aware of this but if he knew what caused the delay of seven years he kept it a secret.[34] Racial consciousness may well have been one of the factors. There had been some enthusiasm for a German province and the opposite viewpoint probably did not lack exponents. Accidentally the day of the conferring of the pallium became exceptionally memorable for Heiss. Archbishop Purcell of Cincinnati was to officiate but he took sick and Heiss substituted for him. Then, too, only a few days earlier Heiss had consecrated Rupert Seidenbusch, O.S.B., in St. Cloud because Henni still lacked the pallium.[35]

After patriarchal Henni had the pallium, he started to crumble under the weight of his years. A coadjutor was needed. Because there was as yet no apostolic delegate in the United States and since there had been no plenary council recently, this proposal involved much individual initiative. All archbishops were informed of the projected change so that they could advise the Vatican.[36] Bishop Grace of St. Paul wrote to Archbishop Gibbons of Baltimore on September 8, 1878, concerning the meeting of the bishops of the province of Milwaukee: "Of the six bishops present at the convention, including the archbishop, I was the only one not German. It was with the utmost difficulty I succeeded in obtaining the consent of the bishops to hear the name of an

---

[34]Salzmann to the Ludwig Mission Society, July 31, 1867, *Salesianum*, April, 1947, p. 67, says that Milwaukee was proposed as an archdiocese at the second plenary council of Baltimore. Same to same, May 3, 1873, *Salesianum*, Oct., 1947, p. 173, says Rome seems to have received favorably the petition that Milwaukee be made a German province. Heiss to Kleiner, June 22, 1867, *Salesianum*, July, 1916, p. 20.

[35]Heiss to Kleiner, June 19, 1875, *Salesianum*, July, 1917, pp. 14-15.

[36]Heiss to Woelfle, April 29, 1878, *Salesianum*, Jan., 1918, p. 28.

American prelate proposed as one of the candidates for the appointment. The prelate is the Rt. Rev. Bishop Spalding of Peoria, Ill. .... The Very Rev. M. Kundig, vicar general of the archdiocese, came to me the evening before the convention to urge me for the sake of religion to do all in my power to have the name of Bishop Spalding on the list of candidates ... I have been told that Your Grace has already been informed of this condition of things in the archdiocese of Milwaukee and throughout Wisconsin, where all the three present bishops are Germans. It is to be feared there will be little or no change in the present policy in the archdiocese if either of the German candidates on the list should receive the appointment of coadjutor. They are intensely German, as indeed are also the other bishops of the province of Milwaukee .... I share in the opinion of the V. G. Kundig, the oldest and most respected among the German priests of the archdiocese, that the appointment of a coadjutor who will be likely to change the existing policy and give a different tone to the Church in Wisconsin, is of vital importance to the interests of religion and the advancement of the Church. A very large proportion of the Wisconsin clergy, both German and English speaking — the really worthy and intelligent — are, I am assured, of the same sentiments."[37]

A year and a half elapsed before Rome selected the coadjutor. Much happened in a period which might pass for mere procrastination. Within a few weeks after the matter was broached a violent controversy had arisen.

First the rumor spread that the Propaganda favored a native American for Milwaukee. More likely than not, this preference originated on this side of the sea. Next some alleged that Heiss was sickly. Henni rebutted that if he could not have Heiss he would continue without help.[38] From the Milwaukee archdiocese itself came protests against Heiss which had been sent

---

[37]Daniel F. Reilly, *The School Controversy (1891-1893)* (Washington, 1943), p. 248.

[38]Heiss to Kleiner, July 16, 1879, *Salesianum*, Jan., 1918, pp. 30-1.

to the new archbishop of Baltimore by men like G. Willard, P. F. Pettit, H. F. Fairbanks, T. Fagan, E. J. Fitzpatrick and M. Kundig.[39] Gibbons took the matter seriously and, after conferring with others of high rank, advised Cardinal Simeoni that Spalding was the most worthy of the candidates.

In the interim the secular press carried anonymous reports that Heiss was deficient in English grammar and that he blundered in his public statements. Father Fagan of the seminary faculty, rightly or wrongly, came under suspicion of authoring some of them. The German professors were accused of having petitioned Rome for a German coadjutor but *Columbia* scotched the charge by publishing a signed statement from them. Henni put the quietus on the literary battle on January 19, 1879, by writing a letter to the clergy forbidding any further newspaper controversy.

"Lamentable efforts", wrote Henni, "were made to destroy the blessed peace and harmony of our archdiocese by arousing the national feelings of the faithful . . . . . Those articles were written in a tone and manner that call for our severest rebuke. It looked, indeed, as though we had been on the eve of a political election and some unscrupulous demagogue had used his venomous pen wantonly to heap insults and stains upon a candidate not to his taste and even to defame anyone suspected of being in his favor . . . . .

"In particular we want to point out and emphasize the unmanly and unchristian spirit in which our seminary, our pride and joy, has been again and again misrepresented. It has been stated repeatedly that 'its German professors have signed, circulated and sent a petition for a German coadjutor to Rome', but never even the least proof for this assertion has been given, though emphatically called for. We felt it our duty to investigate into the matter. And now, after a most careful investigation of our own, we are fully convinced that the above assertion is entirely

---

[39] John Tracy Ellis, *The Life of James Cardinal Gibbons Archbishop of Baltimore 1834-1921* (Milwaukee, 1952), vol. I, pp. 336-339.

false and must stigmatize this attack on our dearest institution as slanderous and dishonorable . . . . .

"We condemn the priests who, in a public newspaper, hold up the character and actions of a bishop to the contempt and criticism of an often prejudiced multitude! And this has been done in those articles — with regard to the Rt. Rev. Bishop of La Crosse, our dear friend and faithful co-laborer for thirty-five years in this state of Wisconsin — to him who is alike distinguished for his great piety, deep learning, and ardent zeal for our holy religion. We hereby do most severely disapprove and condemn the insults heaped upon him by those articles . . . . . It is altogether contrary to all the rules of our holy Church to appeal for a decision in such a matter from the hierarchy of the Church to the laity and thus to make public opinion or rather natural feelings the arbiter in deciding who is to govern the Church of Christ."

On the other side of the ocean friends such as Cardinal Hergenroether[40] did not forget Heiss in their dealings with the Propaganda. Finally, on March 15, 1880, the decisive cablegram reached Milwaukee. Heiss, triumphant yet timorous, wrote: "The opposition party which had powerful patrons in Rome tried everything to prevent my appointment . . . . . The opposition is silenced but whether the minds are changed I am unable to tell."

When the coadjutor arrived in Milwaukee he did not live with Archbishop Henni but at his old home, the seminary.[41] Some of the professors had been unfriendly to him, so not all were elated with his coming. Soon, however, the new coadjutor had the pleasure of consecrating the fourth rector the second bishop of La Crosse. Like himself, Flasch was a Bavarian im-

---

[40] Heiss to Kleiner, April 27, 1880, *Salesianum*, April, 1918, p. 20.

[41] Heiss wrote to Marty after becoming coadjutor that the debts of the archdiocese required a payment of $3,000 a year in interest. He boarded at the seminary because he had no means to use for living expenses. Peter J. Rahill, *The Catholic Indian Missions and Grant's Peace Policy 1870-1884* (Washington, 1953), pp. 310-311.

migrant.[42] The ceremony took place on August 24, 1881, in the seminary chapel with Bishops Krautbauer of Green Bay and Seidenbusch of northern Minnesota serving as co-consecrators.

On the following September 7 the venerable Archbishop Henni died. Heiss offered the Mass of requiem on the tenth. Since the latter had the right of succession there was no interregnum, but even before assuming the hegemony he had dithyrambically taken issue with a number of irregularities. He gave the financial condition of the diocese priority. In a letter to the clergy dated December 20, 1880, he disclosed that the diocesan income had not even been meeting the interest on the diocesan debt. To remedy this he proposed that each priest give on the average fifty dollars per year for the next four years. If some could not afford that much, others might be able to contribute more to maintain the average. These payments would take the place of the cathedraticum. Other sources would be tapped for the support of the archbishop. Priests were urged to make their payments immediately, if possible, and they were allowed to solicit the help of their parishioners in meeting the payments.

On January 21, 1881, he sent out a circular stressing the need for parochial schools and cautioning priests not to absolve parents who did not patronize them. He deplored the increase of mixed marriages, reminded pastors of their obligation to publish the banns, and he admonished those applying for dispensations to state whether the non-Catholic person was baptized.

Picnics, fairs, and excursions needed the express permission of the archbishop because of the abuses connected with them. Such permission would never be given for Sundays or holy days of obligation.

Priests were forbidden to buy vestments or sacred vessels on credit. If they did, they were personally liable for the payments.

---

[42]Flasch, born in 1831, came to America in 1847, studied at Notre Dame University, and transferred to St. Francis when it opened. He was ordained in 1859. He did some pastoral work but was mostly at the seminary where he succeeded Wapelhorst as rector. He died on Aug. 3, 1891.

Nor were pastors to spend more than $300 without the written approval of the bishop as required by the council of Baltimore. Then, too, the ten dollars pledged at the retreat for the support of infirm priests should be paid promptly.

A year later he announced that the pallium would be bestowed upon him on Sunday, April 23, 1882. Bishop Ireland would preach the sermon. After reviewing the accomplishments of his predecessor, Heiss referred somewhat ambiguously to the financial status of St. Francis Seminary and pointed out that the Catholic Normal School was unique in the United States and deserving of all possible support. He regretted that some Catholics still did not see the need for parochial schools, and he lamented the absence of an industrial school for wayward youths but the expense of establishing one was prohibitive.

Archbishop Henni had been opposed to receiving contributions directly from the laity, consequently there was no cathedraticum until Heiss introduced it. Originally he had planned to do this at a diocesan synod but since he could not obtain the necessary modifications of the canonical formalities he contented himself with merely announcing this innovation in a circular letter dated August 10, 1885. Heiss proposed that each parish pay 25 cents per family annually and that the clergy remit five percent of the stole fees plus five percent of all collections. Though less than other dioceses paid it would suffice. He further complained that he had no chancery office and he pointed out that Monsignor Batz, his vicar general, gave his service without remuneration. The archbishop said his conscience forbade him to continue that way, but the proximate cause of the change lay in the recent council of Baltimore which had touched upon such administrative matters.

The letter remarked that in concert with the other Wisconsin bishops he had succeeded in having the legislature pass an act for incorporating church property. The laws were entirely satisfactory but executing and applying them would require considerable work. Respecting diocesan finances he said: "Five years ago when I came to Milwaukee the archdiocese and the cathedral were burdened with a heavy debt. It amounted to $77,000. My first step toward liquidation consisted in separating the debts of the cathedral from those of the diocese. After a careful analysis of the debt I regarded it as proper for the cathedral to assume $26,000 leaving $51,000 on the diocese. To preserve this separation I had to give the cathedral its own administration like that of any other parish, and it became necessary for me to live in a house entirely separate from the cathedral. This was accomplished without expense to the archdiocese. . . The cathedral parish has liquidated its whole debt and the debt on the archdiocese was reduced to $10,000." Thanks to the cooperation of the priests and their parishioners this residue was paid by 1887.[43]

While Milwaukee was becoming solvent the bishops of the country were thinking about convoking a plenary council. Originally Cardinal McCloskey of New York, Archbishop Wood of Philadelphia, and Archbishop Gibbons of Baltimore opposed the idea but Archbishop Heiss canvassed the opinions of the western bishops and informed Gibbons on August 26, 1881, that they favored a council.[44] Accordingly, the Holy See summoned the archbishops to Rome in 1883 to arrange the agenda. Upon arriving they found the outline of the council already sketched but at their insistence the original draft was modified by the joint action of the cardinals and archbishops.

In the course of these preliminary deliberations Heiss raised the question who should judge whether a given school is a proximate danger to the faith. He believed the bishop should decide but wondered whether confessors could do so in individual cases. The cardinals answered that when it came to judging the school the bishop should make the decision; confessors could decide whether this or that person were jeopardizing his faith by attending. Heiss further queried whether bishops could prohibit

---

[43] Harry H. Heming, *The Catholic Church in Wisconsin* (Milwaukee, 1898), p. 305.

[44] Francis P. Cassidy, "Catholic Education in the Third Plenary Council of Baltimore", *Catholic Historical Review*, Oct., 1948, p. 261.

attendance at public schools solely because this would undermine Catholic schools. The response was negative.[45]

At the council itself Heiss and his suffragans campaigned for standardizing the courses in seminaries. Though difficult of attainment, they favored founding chairs of philosophy and theology and introducing uniform courses of two and four years respectively. Probably stimulated by the traditions of Wapelhorst and Singenberger the Milwaukee prelates wanted courses in liturgy and chant. On the other hand, they opposed sending seminarians to villas for their vacations. Operating such estates involved considerable expense, parents would discourage vocations if their sons were kept in exile from home, and hermetically sealing a young man off from the world and then suddenly returning him to it could be disastrous.[46]

In drafting legislation on parish schools some prelates preferred to "advise" or "admonish" parents to send their children. Others favored severe phraseology. Heiss, for one, feared that if the word "command" were dropped Catholic schools currently operating would suffer. On the other hand, where they did not exist such sternness could cause no harm.[47]

Heiss served on at least three committees: he was one of the group designated to define accurately just what constitutes a Catholic school, and he belonged to the permanent committee to unify the examinations and curricula of seminaries. This latter work was to be undertaken only after consulting the colleges in Rome, Louvain, and Innsbruck. As a member of the committee on new business he eventually came under suspicion. Neither he, who definitely wanted the council to convene, nor the other Ger-

---

[45] *Ibid.*, p. 270. He also proposed that only five feast days be holy days of obligation. "Minutes of the Roman Meeting Preparatory to the Third Plenary Council of Baltimore", *The Jurist*, July, 1951, p. 420.

[46] *Ibid.*, p. 271. The villa idea was not new to Heiss. In his memoirs he referred to keeping the students at Eichstaett for vacation.

[47] *Ibid.*, p. 302. Enzlberger, writing to James McMaster, Piopolis, Ill., Dec. 14, 1884, quoted an aphorism of Heiss: "The school question is the question of life for our Church in America." Ms. in Notre Dame University archives.

man bishops raised the question of German grievances in spite of the fact that Gibbons submitted to this committee the question of the canonical rights of German parishes operating in St. Louis.[48]

After the plenary council adjourned Heiss convoked a provincial council in Milwaukee to promulgate the decisions of Baltimore. The Milwaukee gathering lasted from May 23 to 30, 1886, and included five bishops: Seidenbusch and Marty, both of whom were Benedictines; Ireland, Vertin, and Flasch; Father Katzer, the administrator of Green Bay, and Abbot Edelbrock of St. John's in Minnesota.

Though apparently a perfunctory sequel to the national prototype, the meetings were factious because the demand for making St. Paul an archdiocese grew from day to day. Why gather, then, with the metropolitan of Milwaukee to discuss matters which would soon be withdrawn from his supervision? On the other hand, Heiss wanted the decrees approved and promulgated before the change took place. Besides the strained relations between Ireland and his superior, tension existed between Heiss and Marty. The latter had written to Rome requesting that his vicariate of Dakota be split into two dioceses and be made dependent upon St. Paul. He had been losing too much time going to Milwaukee where he found neither sympathy nor understanding of his problems. Then, too, Bishop Seidenbusch was the center of some storms in Minnesota which culminated in his resignation.[49] Many factors, therefore, conspired to make St. Paul an archdiocese as soon as the Milwaukee decrees were approved.

---

[48]*Ibid.*, part II, Jan., 1949, p. 415; part I, p. 281. Rainer in his *Diary*, July 7, 1885, records going to Buffalo where Heiss and other bishops held a conference to regulate studies in seminaries. Ms. in Salzmann Library, St. Francis, Wis.

Before Dwenger took the acts of the council to Rome, Heiss wrote to him from Milwaukee, Feb. 19, 1885, saying that he had no special wishes concerning his diocese. Heiss had asked Simeoni for a dispensation regarding synods because it was impossible to call all priests together who had the care of souls. Heiss expected Dwenger to support this request in Rome. Ms. in Notre Dame University archives.

[49]James H. Moynihan, *The Life of Archbishop John Ireland* (New York, 1953), pp. 14-19.

Though the Milwaukee council marshaled a sizable list of prominent men, its final legislation is languid. Of local interest is a word of commendation for the Catholic Normal School and the Caecilia Society. Heiss, incidentally, was an excellent singer owing partly to the fact that he had studied violin and flute in his school days. Young priests, the council decreed, were to be examined for five years in the sacred sciences and their faculties would be doled out in one year terms. Parish missions were endorsed but the concomitant collections ought not to be unduly exalted nor were new devotions to be introduced without the bishop's consent.

The council fixed the fee for dispensations at $2.00. The discussion on clerical support culminated in dividing pastors into two classes. One received $1,000 per year; the other $800. They had no right to the collections, but the parishes had to defray the expenses incurred in divine worship. The Easter and Christmas collections[50] were reserved for good causes specified by the ordinary. The salary of assistants was contingent: the pastor and curate were to make an agreement between themselves pending the ordinary's approval. Though this problem may have been acute, it was rare because few pastors had curates. Presuming that the latter were not always welcome, the council went on record as endorsing their presence in parishes of four hundred or more families.

Respecting catechetical instruction the council decreed that children of advanced age should study the catechism *also* in English even if they normally used another language. Bishop Marty contrived to insert this into the decrees by averring that thousands of Germans forsook the Church because religion was not taught in English as a preparation for the use of that language in religious services. While Marty, himself a German-speaking Swiss, ac-

---

[50]This rule must have fallen into desuetude at an early date. Katzer in a letter of Dec. 15, 1900, ordering the collection for the orphans wrote: "Where the custom exists that the Christmas collection is an offering for the priest, the collection for the orphans will take place on the following Sunday."

complished this, Ireland later claimed that he wanted to discuss other difficulties connected with the use of German but that the floor was denied him.

The council advised Catholics to avoid labor unions because they were dangerous organizations even though they could be defended in theory. The dangers lay in the possibility of transgressing the limits of justice. Then, too, they tend in the direction of condemned societies, and by bringing together people of different religions or of no religion they promote religious indifferentism. The pastoral letter preached diplomatically to both the employers and the employes: "When capitalists follow the heathen rule to buy labor on the cheapest market God is not with them; and when laborers imagine that all men should have an equal share in the comforts and enjoyments of this earthly life, Divine Providence has ruled otherwise."

The archbishop himself favored the cause of labor more than many of his contemporaries. When the Knights of Labor were decried as radicals, Socialists, or the equivalent of Freemasons, Heiss examined the organization, gave interviews to its friends, and concluded that it was about the same as a trade union. Therefore it was free from censure.[51] Five years before Leo XIII issued *Rerum Novarum* Heiss said: "I know workingmen are not used right in all respects, and they have a right to unite and combine against the encroachments and hungry monopolists of the country; but they must be law abiding." Heiss' stand differed from that of many German priests in Wisconsin, and he helped to form the national Catholic policy by assuring Gibbons, "I could not find anything that would justify me to put them under the societies absolutely forbidden by the Church."

While the archdiocese was adjusting itself to the decree of Baltimore and ruminating its own new legislation, the projected national university, an outgrowth of the third plenary council, was approaching viabiliy. With Gibbons and Ireland backing this venture, Heiss naturally remained cool to it. With Spalding guid-

---

[51] Henry J. Browne, *The Catholic Church and the Knights of Labor* (Washington, 1949), pp. 135-7, 212-3, 321.

ing intellectual matters, Heiss became cooler. Could he forget the attempts to bar him from the metropolitan throne? Apart from this, Heiss naturally envisioned a glorious future for his normal school and seminary. Such an outlook automatically aligned him with Bishop McQuaid of Rochester who was tirelessly promoting St. Bernard's Seminary and deprecating the University.

Heiss maintained that all seminaries should be improved. Thereby the wishes of the Holy See would be satisfied.[52] Having known Reisach and having spent the prime of his life in seminary work, Heiss endorsed this kind of training. Bishop Spalding, however, said publicly and bluntly at the council of Baltimore that a seminary is not an instrument of culture. "It must impart a certain amount of professional knowledge, fit its students to become more or less expert catechists, rubricists, and casuists, and its aim is to do this, and whatever mental improvement, if any thence results, is accidental . . . . Its textbooks are written often in a barbarous style, the subjects are discussed in a dry and mechanical way, and the professor, wholly intent upon giving instruction, is indifferent as to the manner in which it is imparted, or else, not possessing himself a really cultivated intellect, he holds in slight esteem expansion and refinement of mind, looking upon it as at best a mere ornament. . . . If its course were lengthened to five, to six, to eight, to ten years, its students would go forth to their work with more thorough professional training, but not with more really cultivated minds."[53]

Heiss wrote to Gibbons on May 17, 1884, "The proposal for a 'Catholic University' or rather for a higher 'Seminary for Philosophy and Theology' has been made by Rt. Rev. Bishop Grace, without having much support from the majority of the bishops; the most of them are of the opinion all that can be done now would be to improve the studies of our larger or provincial seminaries."[54]

---

[52]Cassidy, art. cit., p. 272.
[53]The Memorial Volume A History of the Third Plenary Council of Baltimore (Baltimore, 1885), p. 92 of the sermons.
[54]John Tracy Ellis, The Formative Years of the Catholic University of America (Washington, 1946), p. 95.

Despite his dissuasive report, Heiss was appointed to the university committee in 1884. However, he declined to attend even the first formal meeting the following May. Rumors of discord found their way into the secular press, but as late as October 24, 1885, Heiss wrote to Gibbons that John Lawler[55] of Prairie du Chien would donate $5,000 or more to the university and he delegated Bishop Ireland to serve as his proxy at the next committee meeting. On April 17, 1886, Heiss tendered his resignation. After that, Bishop Marty passed as the strategic man to stimulate interest for the university among the Germans.

The tension that the university project revealed had long been accumulating. Its cause was nationalism. Throughout the history of the American Church, starting in the remote days of Bishop Carroll, racial consciousness played a conspicuous role alternating between the foreground and the background. Never was it more conspicuous than in the second last decade of the nineteenth century.

In 1883, five years after Spalding's candidacy for Milwaukee, John Gilmary Shea, the well-known historian, published an article in the *American Catholic Quarterly Review* castigating nationalism in the Church and the lack of "American" bishops in the West. The *Pastoral-Blatt* promptly carried a rebuttal: "Clerical Knownothingism in the Catholic Church". Parenthetically it may be remarked that midway between the two articles Peter Paul Cahensly arrived in the new world.[56] He was both a German statesman and a pivotal man in the St. Raphael Society for the protection of immigrants. After returning to Europe he took part in conferences which tried to determine how many Catholics had defected from the Faith. Even today there is no reliable information on this subject but everyone concedes great losses. Sixty years ago few admitted this. Those who advanced such claims

---

[55] *Ibid.*, p. 163.

[56] The mysteriousness which used to envelop Cahensly has been dispelled by Colman Barry, *The Catholic Church and German Americans* (Milwaukee, 1953). See also "Minutes of the Roman Meeting Preparatory to the Third Plenary Council of Baltimore", *The Jurist*, October, 1951, p. 539.

then were assumed to be assailing the hierarchy. This assumption of hostility was not entirely baseless because a number of people had alleged that the apostasies resulted from the desire of some ordinaries to accelerate the natural process of Americanization by not appointing German priests in German settlements. Sanguine proponents of this theory magnified this and minimized other causes of defection such as the original laxity of many immigrants in their homelands.

More exasperating than the diagnosis were the therapeutic recommendations from abroad. The Europeans urged the multiplication of national parishes, the teaching of religion in foreign languages, the founding of parochial schools for every nationality, the increase of mutual aid societies, and the inclusion of bishops of every nationality in the hierarchy.

These recommendations produced the loudest repercussions in the year that Heiss died. But returning to the controversy of 1883 between Shea and the *Pastoral-Blatt* recalls that the next step in the conflict was the petition of eighty-two German-American priests of St. Louis to Rome asking that national parishes be placed on a canonical par with the others. This document was dated July 31, 1884, that is, shortly before the council of Baltimore convened. On October 2, 1885, Bishop Gilmour of Cleveland and Bishop Moore of St. Augustine drew up a counterblast for the Propaganda entitled *Memoriale sulla questione dei Tedeschi nella chiesa di America*. This denounced German egoism and demanded more Irish bishops.

Gilmour said he knew what efforts had been made to secure German bishops for Columbus and Vincennes. The Germans were promoting Bishop Dwenger of Fort Wayne for St. Louis. The bishop of Detroit acclaimed Bishop Richter of Grand Rapids as another German bishop. The Germans wanted Cincinnati but no one cared to accept it because of its condition. There was some speculation about making Vincennes an archdiocese, which, again, the Germans hoped to control. As for Milwaukee, Gilmour and Moore testified: "We have heard it said and we regard it as true that the archbishop of Milwaukee, Msgr. Heiss, asserted that no Irishman would ever occupy his throne." Other pertinent parts of the *Memoriale* read:

"The number of German bishops is actually no longer in proportion to the number of Catholic Germans so that at present it seems that one is trying to Germanize the Church in the United States. For example, in the provinces of Cincinnati and Milwaukee there are seventeen bishops. Of these, nine are German and only one is Irish. Of the ten bishops of the province of Cincinnati not one is Irish. An attempt was made to remedy this injustice and Irish priests were nominated for Nashville, Covington, and Grand Rapids—they were the first on the list, and, none the less, in all three cases they were not accepted and a German priest, always the last on the list, was picked. . . . The Irish priests show themselves determined to insist that the Irish priests will have their proportionate part in the episcopate and that the state of affairs in Milwaukee and Cincinnati will not be repeated. . . . In future the Irish will have to receive better care and the Irish priests of the West should have a better share in the episcopate, otherwise we will see the Catholic body divided in the United States into Irish and German whence will result scandals and the loss of faith and of souls."

It is impossible to say precisely when Heiss became familiar with the *Memoriale,* but in October 1886 he approved Father Abbelen's[57] *Relatio de questione germanica* with a laconic *"Legi et approbavi".* Abbelen, being somewhat familiar with the hierarchy because he had served as Heiss' theologian at the council of Baltimore, wheedled a letter of introduction out of Cardinal Gibbons and then set out for the Vatican. Abbelen may have been backed more in St. Louis than in Milwaukee but Heiss made the controversy his own by his approbation. The *Relatio* was not a point by point rebuttal of the *Memoriale* but it referred to

---

[57] Abbelen came from the diocese of Muenster. He heard Salzmann plead for priests and came to America in 1866. Henni ordained him in 1868. For a few months he taught in the seminary and then accompanied Heiss to La Crosse. After doing pastoral work he became chaplain at Notre Dame Convent in Milwaukee, a monsignor, and a vicar general. He died in 1917.

the grievances of German parishes and recommended that all churches be on an equal footing with the English parishes and be entirely independent of them. Immigrants from Europe were to be assigned to churches of their own languages; bishops and priests were not to uproot the language and devotional customs of the Germans, and those who governed mixed dioceses should appoint a German as well as an Irish vicar general.

The Heiss-Abbelen petition reached Rome a few months after Gibbons had become a cardinal. So it was well known that he, whose opinion differed radically from theirs, stood high in the Church's inmost circles. More important still was the fact that it arrived just when Bishop Ireland and Bishop Keane of Richmond were there adjusting matters concerning the embryonic University. These two confidants of Gibbons immediately denounced the *Relatio* to Cardinal Simeoni, the prefect of the Propaganda, and, as the news of their action spread like ripples on a pond, other bishops lent moral support. Their document blandly denied the existence of any quarrel between the Irish and the Germans. Rather unconvincingly it alleged that the difference was solely one of language. It berated conditions in La Crosse and Green Bay as well as in Milwaukee while it attributed to Henni the same statement that Heiss allegedly made, namely, that no Irishman would ever occupy the throne of Milwaukee.

Simultaneously, that is early in 1887, the Priesterverein came into existence. It probably gave resonance to the views of Abbelen and Heiss but it attracted many members in the St. Louis area from which its first president, Father Muehlsiepen, came.[58] In Milwaukee an antipode took the name American Catholic Clerical Union. The latter elicited praise from Ireland in a letter to his friend O'Connell.[59] Its admitted objective was to "maintain the rights, privileges, and standing of the English speaking clergy, and to foster and guard the English laity of the province of Milwaukee. For this purpose it will use all just and honorable

---

[58]Barry, *op. cit.*, p. 98.
[59]*Ibid.*, p. 126.

means to obtain a fair and equal representation of English speaking bishops, officials in dioceses, and priests in congregations throughout the province."[60]

The intrigues of these groups led the *Catholic Review* of New York to denounce all clerical unions. By contrast the future Archbishop Messmer, then a professor of canon law at the Catholic University, defended such organizations[61] which, in practice if not in theory, could hamper a bishop in governing his diocese.

In August of 1887, shortly before the annual convention of the Central Verein, Heiss gave an interview to a reporter of the Milwaukee *Sentinel*.[62] Though not planning to attend the convention, he chatted about the projected Leo House at New York for German immigrants. Long ago he had expected the German language to become extinct in America when the old people died but, to his surprise, the demand for it had steadily increased. The reporter queried:

"Do the German Catholics and the German priests feel that they are entitled to a greater recognition in the appointment of bishops and archbishops?"

Heiss answered: "There are some that undoubtedly feel that way, but such matters cannot always be helped. We ought to have a few more, but then we are not so particular."

"What is the proportion of German Catholics in America?"

"There are," said he, "about 8,000,000 Catholics in the United States, and of these 3,000,000 are Germans. But out of twelve archbishops and sixty bishops, only one archbishop (myself) and eleven bishops are German."

Then Heiss went over the hierarchy and pointed out the nationality of each member. This proved to be extremely irritating yet he neither appraised the man nor his nationality. He ended his analysis by remarking: "You see the Germans are not

---

[60] Quoted in John Gmeiner, *The Church and Foreignism* (St. Paul, 1891), p. 35.

[61] Barry, *op. cit.*, pp. 125-127.

[62] August 18, 1887.

very numerous and if it wasn't for the Milwaukee province, they wouldn't cut any figure whatever. Of course, I can't speak of any dissatisfaction among the Germans in my own province."

The reporter continued: "In what province beside Milwaukee do the Germans predominate?"

"In those of St. Louis and Cincinnati".

"Don't you think that German archbishops will be appointed in both these provinces as soon as a vacancy occurs?"

"No, that cannot be taken for granted. The bishops are not German, you know, and they nominate the candidate that is appointed at Rome. Unless the bishops can be persuaded or induced to nominate a German, I do not believe that one will be appointed. The archbishop of St. Louis has been in office fifty years, being appointed at a time when there were comparatively few Germans in the province."

The same year that Heiss gave his analytic interview on national affairs he tried to turn his seminary over to the German Jesuits of the Buffalo mission.[63] Since the seminary figured in the *Memoriale* this may have been a stratagem to make it depend less directly upon the archbishop of Milwaukee and to withdraw it from local clerical controversies such as had occurred when he became coadjutor. It also manifests a deep confidence in the Society of Jesus which, starting already with Novalis' *Europa oder die Christenheit,* characterized many Germans in the past century.

Somewhat related to the question of race was that of liquor. Early in the century New England Protestants started to campaign against the evils of alcohol and Father Mathew's crusade in Ireland set off sympathetic repercussions on this side of the sea. However, when he came in person the hierarchy turned skeptical because he associated with Protestants and fraternized with fanatics. In 1866 the plenary council of Baltimore recommended total abstinence. In this Irish groups took the lead but Bishop Ireland

---

[63]Gilbert J. Garraghan, *The Jesuits of the Middle United States* (New York, 1938), vol. III, pp. 453, 583.

and some others eventually concluded that moral suasion was ineffective. Only the state could save the nation from drunkenness. The third plenary council again endorsed the abstinence movement and struck at saloons and the violation of Sunday rest. No doubt the movement was strong in many places, yet it did not sweep through Wisconsin with its large German element despite the eloquence of Fathers Cleary, Ward, and Willard.

Archbishop Heiss was reported as saying that the German priests would not crusade for closing saloons on Sunday and Abbelen was quoted as saying that they had no objections to allowing the laborer a stein of beer on Sunday in a saloon or beer garden. In a few brusque words Heiss eliminated one annoyance from his mail box by writing to *The Catholic Total Abstinence News* on April 15, 1889: "Please don't send your paper to my address; for though it may be valuable in itself, I cannot find time to read it."[64]

That same year one last crisis was developing. The Bennett law.[65] This piece of legislation, introduced by a Catholic congressman[66] from Iowa county, consisted of fourteen sections and

---

[64] Joan Bland, *Hibernian Crusade The Story of the Catholic Total Abstinence Union of America* (Washington, 1951), pp. 139, 149.

[65] Heming, *op. cit.*, pp. 281-7; Louise Phelps Kellog, "The Bennett Law in Wisconsin", *Wisconsin Magazine of History*, vol. II, pp. 3-25; William F. Whyte, "The Bennett Law Campaign in Wisconsin", *ibid.*, vol. X, pp. 363-390, 455-61; H. G. Riordan, "The Real Hitch in the Bennett Law", *Salesianum*, Aug., 1921, pp. 1-4; W. F. Vilas, "The 'Bennett Law' in Wisconsin", *Forum*, Oct. 1891, pp. 196-207.

As early as Feb. 15, 1840, *The Truth Teller*, edited by an Irish Catholic layman, deplored using any language other than English in schools because any other policy tended to be divisive. Father Varela, a Cuban who edited *The Catholic Register*, agreed. Henry J. Browne, "Public Support of Catholic Education in New York, 1825-1842: Some New Aspects", *Catholic Historical Review*, April, 1953, p. 13.

[66] Michael John Bennett was born in Clyde, Wis., on Jan. 6, 1860. A farmer and teacher, he became town clerk in 1885, and assemblyman in 1887. He claimed that there were two parochial schools in his assembly district in which no English was taught. *Milwaukee Sentinel*, Oct. 28, 1889. *Ibid.*, March 22, 1890, referred to his being a Catholic. Fond du Lac *Commonwealth*, June 20, 1890, reported he was a Catholic in good standing, a member of Father Dempsey's parish, Highland. In 1890 Edmund Baker defeated Bennett 1,196 to 1,043. Thereafter the latter lapsed into obscurity.

had three major objectives: to establish compulsory school attendance, to compel the use of English in schools during a substantial part of the day, and to put restrictions on child labor. These aims were reasonable in themselves but at the time some thought or alleged that the state was preparing to usurp the rights of parents over their children. The law stung particularly because it hindered immigrants from giving their children the kind of education which the parents themselves knew and wanted to pass on to posterity. Educators may argue that the rights of the state to promote the general welfare should take precedence in such matters, but the Bennett law had counterparts in Massachusetts and other states and it must be analyzed in conjunction with a general pattern of thought propagated by such groups as the A. P. A. and the Turnvereine. Heiss began the analysis and launched the attack but more he could not do.

Serious sickness had stricken the archbishop as a man of sixty-five when he went to Rome to prepare for the third plenary council of Baltimore. After that he intermittently spoke of retiring but he never stated his reasons clearly. One may have been his physical condition, another his homesickness for Bavaria, a third his conviction that he had solved the financial problems of the diocese, and a fourth may have been the lack of harmony with his fellow rulers in the American church. True, late in life he had pushed for a council but its course and sequel probably baffled and thwarted him. The consciousness of advancing years, failing health, and a feeling of frustration may have spurred him on to his last, somewhat reckless, efforts to solve the racial problem. The resultant opposition and ostracism must have crushed all buoyancy out of his spirit.

But despite his mental and physical pains in November 1889 he attended the celebration marking the centenary of the establishment of the American hierarchy. At this event he officiated at pontifical vespers and heard Ireland preach. True to form, the latter included some remarks on patriotism and foreigners. Bishop Katzer, his suffragan at Green Bay, attended as well as Bishop Flasch, his successor in La Crosse. Father Abbelen also made the trip east. Connected with these festivities were the Catholic Congress and the opening of the Catholic University. While Heiss and Flasch attended this last function, Katzer did not. Among the members of the opening class was a representative from the Milwaukee archdiocese, Rev. D. J. O'Hearn. Few dioceses had more; most of them not as many.

Just before Christmas that year Heiss went to La Crosse, to St. Rose Convent, as a sick man. Although he rallied temporarily, he made his last will on February 13. Ten days later he offered Mass for the last time. Meanwhile the Wisconsin hierarchy was formulating its formal protest against the Bennett law. Back in January the Catholics and Lutherans had issued a joint protest, and on March 12, 1890, the official Catholic manifesto appeared over Heiss' signature and those of his suffragans. It was a document that was destined to bring Heiss victory, but, unfortunately for him, he could no longer share in the rare exhilaration of victory.

Early in March Bishop Flasch administered Extreme Unction to him. On March 26, 1890, at 7:45 in the evening the second archbishop of Milwaukee passed into eternity. He was seventy-one years old. To the end he remained a Latinist. In his last hours he told the bystanders: *"Fratres, in proximo est momentum mortis meae. Hoc bene perpendite."*

Archbishop Ireland had the courtesy to attend the obsequies of his neighbor with whom he often had sharply disagreed. Death, however, did not end the disagreement. The survivor took this opportunity to comment favorably on the Bennett law and thereby undermine one of Heiss' last official statements.[67] On March 31 Cardinal Gibbons, always suave, offered a Mass of requiem for him in the cathedral at Milwaukee. The next day, in accordance with the deceased's wish, his remains were interred beneath the chapel of St. Francis Seminary. There they rest

---

[67] Fond du Lac *Commonwealth*, July 18, 1890. For Ireland's defense of the law see Justille McDonald, *History of the Irish in Wisconsin in the Nineteenth Century* (Washington, 1954), p. 175.

near those of Dr. Salzmann and near the sanctuary from which many priests whom he had taught left to do heroic work in a land of hardship and promise. Even today agile levites who know little of his career still walk over his tomb and past his pale marble bust as they go to pray in preparation for their sacred calling.[68]

---

[68]Heiss established a scholarship at the seminary in Eichstaett. When Katzer sent Hengell there he referred to the foundation by Heiss in a letter to the rector dated Sept. 2, 1899. Ms. is at Eichstaett.

II

FREDERICK KATZER

During the Civil War patriarchal Father Pierz, furrowed and gnarled, left Minnesota to visit Austria where he had been born way back in 1785. For three decades he had worked in the American missions. As fervent Father Baraga once had lured him across the sea, now he was enlisting other enthusiasts in the realm of Emperor Francis Joseph for the American missions. Father Buh and fifteen students heard his plea and crossed the Atlantic in 1864. Among them was Frederick Katzer.

He was one of two children born to poor parents in Ebensee. His father, Carl Katzer, had married Barbara Schwarzenbruner on February 6, 1842, when they were 42 and 27 years old respectively. Frederick was born on February 7, 1844, and the next morning Father Hollergschwandtner baptized him. Thirteen months later another son arrived. Soon after that the family moved to Gmunden, the town where the mother had originated.[1]

Here Frederick began to appreciate the beauties of nature and here he received the rudiments of his education. Next he spent several years in a textile factory concurrently attending continuation school. In 1857, with the consent of Bishop Rudigier, he entered the preparatory seminary at Freinberg, near Linz, where he learned to respect the Society of Jesus. He and another lad, Francis M. Doppelbauer,[2] were enabled to pursue their studies by no less a person than the Empress Carolina Augusta, the widow of Emperor Francis I. In addition to this slight contact with high

---

[1] The details of his youth are covered by Franz Loidl, *Erzbischof Friedrich Xaver Katzer Ebensee—Milwaukee 1844-1903* (Vienna, 1953).

[2] Francis M. Doppelbauer was born in 1845. After serving as curate in Steyr he studied at the Anima. In 1879 he became secretary to Bishop Rudigier of Linz; in 1887 rector of the Anima; the following year bishop of Linz. He died in 1908.

society he learned to admire Bishop Rudigier[3] who often visited his seminary to deliver addresses that were characterized by simplicity and severity.

Starting fifteen years before Katzer was born, the Leopoldine Society had been collecting alms for missionaries such as Pierz and Baraga. Although the Austrian lay people shied away from emigrating, their priests went with alacrity to America and other distant parts of the world. In fact, Father Strele, a professor at Freinberg, had gone to Australia to found a mission just a year before Katzer succumbed to the *Wanderlust*.

After receiving a grant from the Leopoldine Society to transport his volunteers, Pierz returned alone to the United States. His disciples landed in New York on May 19, 1864. However, after he had shepherded them into "the promised land" Bishop Grace of St. Paul complained that he had been much too successful. He had enlisted more candidates than the diocese could use. Distressed by this situation, Katzer contemplated going to Baltimore to join the Jesuits. At this juncture of events Dr. Salzmann, a fellow Austrian, invited him to come to St. Francis Seminary and assured him adoption into the Milwaukee diocese. Without delay he parted company with Pierz, banished Minnesota from his mind, and settled permanently in Wisconsin.

On December 21, 1866, Bishop Henni ordained him a priest. A few days later he offered his first Mass in Hartford, Wisconsin. Though he retreated from the ideals of St. Ignatius by joining the secular clergy, like a Jesuit, he mounted the rostrum of the seminary as a professor.[4] This upstart, 22 years old, could not have

---

[3]Francis Joseph Rudigier was born in 1811. After teaching in Brixen he became court chaplain and instructor to Francis Joseph and Maximilian of Mexico. In 1850 he became a canon at Brixen and two years later bishop of Linz. His pastoral letter on education and marriage, issued in 1868, was confiscated. Though prosecuted and convicted, the emperor pardoned him. He died in 1884. The preliminary steps to his canonization have been taken.

[4]In 1867 he had his parents move to America. His brother also came. While Katzer was professor his parents lived at the seminary. They went along with him to Green Bay where his father died in 1876. His mother died in the archiepiscopal residence in Milwaukee in 1895.

had much to offer his hearers, but a seminary only ten years old and near the frontier kept its requirements as modest as its recompense. As a deacon he had taught mathematics; now he added philosophy and dogmatic theology to his repertoire.

In 1871 he went abroad with Father Zeininger,[5] an Austrian co-laborer on the faculty. After this excursion he taught four more years. In that time he organized the Albertus Magnus Verein to foster love of German literature among the students and he published an allegorical drama, *Der Kampf der Gegenwart* (1873). The play, dedicated to his unforgettable professors at Freinberg, glorified the Jesuits and diagnosed Europe's social problems. The proceeds, no doubt modest, he assigned to the Catholic Normal School which Salzmann had just established close to the seminary.

In 1875 the Holy See appointed Father Krautbauer, the chaplain of the School Sisters of Notre Dame, bishop of Green Bay. The latter had emigrated from Bavaria to Buffalo in 1850. Nine years later he came to Milwaukee. Being at the motherhouse of an influential organization gave him easy entree to circles of the clerical elite and apparently Krautbauer took a liking to Katzer. At all rates, he took the professor along to Green Bay where he made him rector of the cathedral and later vicar general.

Hardly had Katzer arrived when the cornerstone of a new cathedral was laid on October 6, 1876. Two years later the basement was completed. On Sunday, November 20, 1881, Bishop Krautbauer consecrated the new red brick structure, dedicated to St. Francis Xavier, while Bishops Flasch and Seidenbusch consecrated the side altars. Archbishop Heiss sang the pontifical high Mass and Bishop Ireland, who passed as the Chrysostom of the midwest, presided in the pulpit. Though the dimensions of the building were modest, it had elegant proportions. This might

---

[5] Augustine Zeininger was born in Linz in 1846. He heard Salzmann's plea for priests and came to America in 1866. He became professor and rector of St. Francis Seminary. He returned to Austria in 1899.

be due to the fact that St. Louis Church in Munich provided the basic pattern.[6]

In 1884 Katzer built a new school in Green Bay, and on December 17 of the following year Bishop Krautbauer died suddenly. In fact, he was found dead in bed. Thereupon Katzer served as administrator of the see and in this capacity he participated in the provincial council of Milwaukee. On July 13, 1886, the Vatican named him bishop of Green Bay, and on September 21, 1886, Archbishop Heiss, assisted by Bishops Vertin of Marquette and Ireland of St. Paul, consecrated him in Green Bay. The mitre was a gift of Notre Dame University.[7] In designing his coat of arms the new ordinary memorialized both his fatherland and his instructors; the upper field showed the Traunsee, the left field a tower at Freinberg.

Becoming bishop, as he did, when the council of Baltimore belonged to recent history meant that he would still have to execute some of its regulations. Among them was the obligation of supporting indigent priests. The council had ordered all ordinaries to discuss this matter and it suggested that mutual aid societies might provide the solution to the problem. Accordingly, on December 13, 1887, Katzer issued a letter[8] directing all priests either to join the St. Leo Benevolent Association or remit $25.00 to the chancery office and $15.00 each year thereafter. Priests who refused to join the society or make the payments would automatically forfeit their claims to support if they became unable to hold a position. In this way Katzer, indeed, made a start but the organization demanded much attention from his successor.

In the spring of 1888 the new bishop left for Austria. After a brief visit to the old haunts he went to Rome to make his *ad*

---

[6] Theodore Roemer, "Munich and Green Bay", *Salesianum*, April, 1940, p. 78.

[7] Notre Dame often showed such courtesies to build good will for its museum. Katzer to ND, Green Bay, Aug. 5, 1886, says he prefers a Gothic mitre and gives his hat size as 6⅞. Katzer to ND, Green Bay, Sept. 24, 1886, expresses thanks for the mitre. Some commented that it was small but he observed that he was short whereas the other bishops were tall.

[8] This is referred to in a circular letter of Messmer, Jan. 13, 1896.

limina. Father Doppelbauer, his old schoolmate who had just been appointed rector of the Anima, did everything to make his stay in Rome pleasant. Nor was the journey fruitless for Zeininger. In the course of the summer he could exchange his black cassock for the regalia of a domestic prelate. After finishing his affairs at the Vatican Katzer went to Linz and from this hub he made excursions to places that interested him. Among them was Gmunden where he had grown up. Here it was his pleasure to visit his old school and Mr. Czech, one of his teachers who was then living in retirement. He also went to Ebensee, his birthplace, where he met Father Hollergschwandtner who had baptised him 44 years ago, and in the course of his stay he gave an address on the social question.

With a view to getting students of theology and members of religious orders for his polyglot diocese he continued on to Hungary, Galicia, and Bohemia. Although his success was slight, he did recruit one Bohemian and two Polish priests, and on August 23 the Leopoldine Society allocated 1000 gulden for their transportation. Moreover, he enlisted six girls from Bavaria for the convent adjoining the seminary at St. Francis.

Katzer likewise received little aid from the Ludwig Mission Society in Bavaria. He obtained one donation of 2400 marks for the general needs of the diocese and on another occasion he asked the society to pay the fare to the United States for A. Belle of Liège and B. Hugenroth of Innsbruck, two theologians who were soon to be ordained priests.[9]

The year following his trip to Europe he held a synod and, taking a cue from Archbishop Heiss, he separated the affairs of the cathedral from those of the diocese. During his brief episcopate of four years the number of schools rose from 44 to 69 and the enrollment jumped from 5292 to 10,785. Part of this development must have been due to the chief shepherd of the flock.

But it was in 1890 that Katzer became known throughout Wisconsin and the nation for his vigorous stand on education.

---

[9] Roemer, *art. cit.*, p. 79.

Early that year Archbishop Heiss was still alive to lend his prestige and give his signature to the document that opened the Catholic drive to repeal the Bennett law. The legislature had enacted this law without fanfare and without opposition in the spring of 1889. However, within a year clever Democratic politicians as well as conservative Lutheran and Catholic leaders queried whether it did not embody a covert attack on basic human rights respecting parental control of the education of children. Cost what it may, Republican Governor Hoard stoutly defended the law and *The Milwaukee Sentinel* lauded it on every possible occasion, yet the movement for repeal had gained much momentum even before Heiss died on March 26, 1890. Though Bishop Flasch of La Crosse had been close to the archbishop during life, this campaign devolved largely upon the bishop of Green Bay. He spoke and wrote about the subject only a few times but apparently his words carried weight with a sizable segment of the electorate.

In May Katzer addressed the first convention of the Wisconsin branch of the Central Verein in Milwaukee.[10] He spoke in German but this did not hinder the English press from giving the speech wide publicity. Said the bishop: "Although we bishops have already spoken. . . . my views on this Bennett law are as follows.[11] It is a step by which the state has transgressed the limits of its powers and arrogated rights which, according to the natural law and a sound philosophy, belong solely to parents. The law is a step which our Church and the other religious societies which still take positive Christianity seriously, must rightly consider as seriously inimical to their interests and welfare. It is a step by which Antichrist is trying to promote its attacks on the Church and accomplish its oppression by the state.

"In order to determine what the rights of the state are, we must not look to Europe. European states have assumed every-

---

[10]Flasch said: "The state has no right to prescribe what is to be taught in our schools. If once granted that privilege it will go farther and assume more. We saw that in Europe." *Milwaukee Sentinel*, May 28, 1890.

[11]*Columbia*, Supplement, May 29, 1890; *Milwaukee Sentinel*, May 28, 1890.

thing imaginable. They have written Hegel's philosophy on their banner according to which the state is the present God and all that it does is divine and right. Naturally, with such principles there are no rights of individuals and families except those which the state has granted and therefore can also withdraw. Should such a monstrous aberration find acceptance in our great republic which proudly calls itself 'The Home of the Free' and should it be incorporated in its laws? We hope not. Here the state is the people and it does not exist without the consent of the individual.

"By nature the lone human being existed before the state. Also his family. After it, then came the state. God created no state but he first created Adam, then Eve. In that way the family began and, in the natural development of things, came the community, namely, the state. God gave rights and duties to the individual and these come first. Next come those of the family. These latter rights certainly cannot annul the earlier ones. The same applies to the rights of the state. It occupies only the third place and has neither the right, nor should it have the power, to touch or impair the rights of the family and the individual. The state has for its purpose to unite families in mutual social relations, to promote their welfare and to protect them in their rights just as it does for individual human beings. Consequently, it goes counter to sound human intelligence if the state assumes rights which belong to the family and the individual.

"But what did the state do when it—let us say it candidly—enacted the Bennett law? It far exceeded the limits of its power by placing the rights of the state over those of the parents. The child belongs to the father who has begotten it and to the mother who bore it nine months and gave birth to it in pain. It belongs to them and not to the state. Just as little as the state has assumed and will not assume for a long time to provide for the corporal development, and for the feeding and clothing of the children, just so little has it a right to determine their education in schools.

"It is asserted that the child has rights and that it is the duty of the state to protect him in his rights. We have heard much of the paternal love which incites our Governor [Hoard] to espouse the cause of the 'poor little German boy'. I don't doubt but that he means it well. But why only and just the 'poor little German boy'? And if he is entirely to enjoy this paternal state providence, why not manifest it also in other ways, such as in food and clothing? Many a one would prefer it, and surely it would be more profitable. And, to view the matter in the light of sound philosophy, what rights does the child have which the state should protect? It has the rights of a human being. These begin with its first breath and the parents to whom it was entrusted must respect them. They are also the natural protectors of them. Only when they obviously neglect their duty has the state a right to interfere. Does the child perhaps have the right to demand: I want to be dressed this way or that way? I want to have this or that to eat? Assuredly not. It can demand from its parents only that clothing and food which they after due deliberation consider beneficial and within their means. Likewise, it can demand from its parents only that education which enables it to succeed later in the world, to become a useful member of society, and, above all, attain its supernatural, eternal destiny. Rights that exceed this it does not possess.

"If the state is so concerned about the child, I would like once more to call attention to the truth that the child enjoys some rights over against the state which the latter must respect. For instance, the child may say to the state: You dare not and cannot compel me to attend a school where I cannot learn and practise my faith. Precisely here the state has encroached upon the rights of the parents. Because Hegel, the pantheist, has declared the state to be God, we do not need to subscribe obediently to his philosophy. In other things we do not align ourselves with Europe, why precisely in this matter which deserves anything but imitation?

"People have accused us of opposing instruction in English. There is here no question of English instruction—we are using more English in our schools than the law demands. Even the district clause comes only secondarily into consideration. Here there is a question of principle, the principle of state control. If we grant this to the state then also it can prescribe—and it will no doubt do it—that we can teach English and nothing else. Foolish people—I almost said something else—go so far as to allow the state to meddle with family affairs. Accordingly, we will next get state commissioners who will dictate to the housewife what she should cook.

"This law is nothing but a blow aimed at the Church, coming from the Free-masons. If I had to adduce direct proofs for this assertion I might find it difficult. But, gentlemen, there is a certain thing which the language of the law calls circumstantial evidence. I think that I can apply it here.

"Occasionally we meet a child or person whose features seem familiar: we should know that nose, the mouth, or the eyes. We think and ponder. Right. The child or person is the son or daughter of this or that family, this or that mother whom we knew well. The similarity and family membership is unmistakable. Now take the Bennett law. There is something about it we know, that we have met elsewhere. It almost agrees with laws of Illinois and Massachusetts; it is similar to laws which we have encountered in Germany, France, and other countries, including Belgium; gag laws against which faithful Catholics rose up. Now, look at all these laws and you will recognize that they are all children of one and the same family, Free-masonry.

"This anti-Christian secret society has for some time been at work to undermine Christianity. The principal weapons which it employed and still employs are: divorce, free love, the abolition of the pope's temporal power, the de-Christianization of the schools, and institutions in which female youth is raised in infidelity and hatred of revealed religion and for the emancipation of women.

"A former Mason told me personally that the underlying principle of the Bennett law, namely, state control of parochial schools, was discussed before the Grand Lodge of Wisconsin already five years ago and such a step was debated. He added: 'I could prove it to you if my life were not too dear to me.' I know the man to whom I refer to be a man of veracity and judgment."

Katzer was very much himself when he castigated the Freemasons.[12] Surely it was not diplomatic to make such remarks precisely when he was trying to win votes for the Democrats and co-ordinate all opposition to the school program of the Republicans. In the terms of the *Iron Port* of Escanaba, a Republican weekly, "The piece kills 'at the breech' rather than at the muzzle".[13] That autumn, just before the election, the *Iron Port*[14] blamed him for arraying Catholics and Protestants against each other thereby justifying the existence of such societies as the A. P. A. The paper quoted him as having said in a sermon at Oshkosh the preceding Sunday that "he personally and officially as bishop of the diocese should consider anyone who did not vote for the repeal of the Bennett law a traitor to the Catholic Church." He made this assertion fully aware of the fact that a coterie of clergy, to say nothing of the laity, failed to discern the iniquity of the Republican legislation.[15]

---

[12]*Antigo Republican,* June 5, 1890, quoted an unsigned letter to the *Green Bay Advocate.* The author, a Mason, said Katzer erred in linking the law to the lodges. Of the 15,000 Masons in Wisconsin, half were Democrats.

[13]June 7, 1890. *Madison Democrat,* May 30, 1890, reported that the convention of Catholic societies was conservative. They allowed compulsory education where parents neglected their duty and they showed no hostility to public schools, but they did not want their schools placed under public school domination.

[14]Nov. 1, 1890.

[15]Father De Kelver of Menasha, a native Wisconsinite of Belgian ancestry, allegedly said the law should have been passed forty years ago. Fond du Lac *Commonwealth,* Oct. 24, 1890. Father Hannan was quoted as saying that English speaking priests everywhere would endorse the law. *Ibid.,* Feb. 14, 1890. *Milwaukee Sentinel,* March 22, 1890, pointed to Irish support of the law. Fond du Lac *Commonwealth,* April 11, 1890, carried a letter from Thomas Kelly. He wrote: "I am a Catholic—an Irish Catholic. I love my church and my religion. But I love this my country better. . . . The German Catholic bishops have issued a circular in which they virtually direct the

Irish groups,[16] for example, recoiled from denouncing the Bennett law for a variety of reasons. Some were not enamored with Archbishop Heiss personally, others, forgetting that they too were immigrants, had become hyper-patriotic singing the praises of the language which they themselves happened to use, and some teachers in the public schools feared the loss of their jobs if the rift between parochial and public schools widened.[17] People in these groups were heartened when the daily papers brought the news of Archbishop Ireland's address to the National Educational Association a month after Katzer's blast at the Bennett law. Here the average man found considerable praise for the public school and for compulsory education while professed Republicans garnered support from the hierarchy's prominent Republican.

Said the archbishop of St. Paul: "I am a friend and an advocate of the state school. In the circumstances of the present time I uphold the parish school. I sincerely wish that the need for it did not exist. I would have all schools for the children of the people to be state schools." He conceded that according to the divine plan parents should rear their children. "But, as things are, tens of thousands of children will not be instructed if parents solely remain in charge of the duty. The state must come forward

---

members of the Catholic Church to vote against any party or man that favors the law. I cannot follow the direction of the German bishops. When they begin to dabble with politics and direct my vote they are out of their province and I will not hear them. In spiritual things they may teach me but I must make my own choices in the field of politics."

[16] Justille McDonald, *History of the Irish in Wisconsin in the Nineteenth Century* (Washington, 1954), pp. 168-181.

The Poles seem to have played a small role. *Milwaukee Sentinel*, March 15, 1890, quoted Mr. Siupecki as saying that the Poles were not against the law. As congressman he had tried to eliminate German from the public schools. The *Sentinel*, Nov. 5, 1890, conceded that the Polish wards voted for Peck. The editor gave due credit to Katzer.

[17] *Shawano County Journal*, Oct. 23, 1890, quoted a speech of C. W. Felker in Milwaukee referring to the Catholics who teach in public schools. It is a sin for Catholic children to attend, said he, but the Church's hypocrisy is evident when she allows her members to teach in them. *Dodgeville Chronicle*, Oct. 24, 1890, quoted Felker as eulogizing the compulsory education laws of Germany and denouncing priests in politics.

as an agent of instruction; else ignorance will prevail. . . . I am unreservedly in favor of state laws making instruction compulsory." And then he touched gently on the Bennett law by remarking that several states had recently enacted compulsory education laws. He endorsed them and found them objectionable only "in their incidental clauses".

Statements such as these might have been dramatically challenged, but the anti-Bennett law movement suffered from the fact that the metropolitan see of Milwaukee remained vacant until after the fall elections. However, just before the election Katzer sent out a letter urging people to vote Democratic[18] and in the end the unique coalition of Lutherans and Catholics swept George W. Peck into the governor's office and the Bennett law into the waste basket.[19]

Meanwhile the politics of the Church threatened to become as raucous as those of the state. Early in the year the bishops of the province proposed as their candidates Katzer of Green Bay, Flasch of La Crosse, and Richter of Grand Rapids. The consultors of the archdiocese also put Katzer in first place. Some English speaking priests of Milwaukee, either suspecting this or knowing it to be a fact, entered mediately into the deliberations by appealing to some archbishops to help them get an English speaking metropolitan. Accordingly when the archbishops of the nation gathered at the first of their annual meetings in Boston they hotly debated the impending appointment. With the exception of Corrigan of New York, all of them opposed Katzer's promotion.[20]

---

[18]*Milwaukee Sentinel*, Nov. 3, 1890. Just before the election Ireland was abundantly quoted and misquoted. *Milwaukee Journal*, Nov. 1, 1890, carried a dispatch saying that he spoke for Minnesota, not Wisconsin.

[19]*North Star*, Marinette, Nov. 6, 1890, commented: "Martin Luther, Pope Leo, and Bill McKinley made a hard combination to down." *Shawano County Journal*, Nov. 6, 1890, fumed: "The Priests Win. . . . It is essentially a church victory, the priests carrying their congregations with them to a man on the Bennett law issue. Never before in this state has religion been so shamefully prostituted in the dirty pool of political strife."

[20]D. F. Reilly, *The School Controversy* (1891-1893) (Washington, 1943), p. 101.

This was merely a repetition of what had happened when Heiss became coadjutor to Henni, but the growth of the Milwaukee archdiocese as well as the widespread discussion of the Bennett law had given this see national prominence. Ireland, who had just attained metropolitan stature, expected to make his influence felt by reason of his rank as well as his proximity, and, since he was not siding with the Wisconsin bishops in the state's gubernatorial campaign, he fumed when he heard of the action of the suffragans and consultors. He told Gibbons that Katzer was "a man thoroughly German and thoroughly unfit to be an archbishop. The Milwaukee question is a most important one for the American church and I will rely on your enlightened cooperation in solving it." So the archbishops again proposed John L. Spalding as their choicest candidate followed by Marty and Richter. Rome apparently restricted its attention to the two lists that came from Wisconsin. If Rome welcomed the archbishops' comments on those names, it ignored their list of candidates.[21]

In December of 1890 the announcement that Katzer had been appointed made known the second defeat of Spalding. Gibbons relayed the news to the new archbishop who—of all things—replied with an allusion to Heiss. "I feel", wrote he, "like a dwarf succeeding a giant. I have not sought the position. I have most reluctantly allowed my name to be put on the list and I have prayed to God to be spared the great responsibility—it comes to pass against my will."[22]

Naturally Katzer's appointment disappointed many people, yet they remained inarticulate when it came to specifically cataloguing his faults. However, the American Catholic Clerical

---

[21]Colman J. Barry, *The Catholic Church and German Americans* (Milwaukee, 1953), pp. 128-130. In Katzer's farewell letter to Green Bay, April 5, 1891, he spoke of Catholic education and urged: "Let no discord, no selfishness, no spirit of nationality arise among you." Bishop Wigger declined the promotion to Milwaukee. *Dictionary of American Biography* s. v. Wigger.

[22]Barry, *Church and German Americans*, p. 129.

Union[23] gathered statistics on the racial and religious composition of the population of Wisconsin. That these suggested gross unfairness goes without saying. After Katzer was appointed the *Milwaukee Sentinel,* whose editor had not forgotten the Bennett law, carried the statistics in full. This was on March 21, 1891. The item observed that many people call Wisconsin a German state but they forget that most Germans are not Catholic. According to the Union, the Catholics who spoke English exceeded the number of those who spoke German, but "of the 16 diocesan consultors in the 4 dioceses only 4 are English speaking . . . .

"While in the diocese of La Crosse the English speaking Catholics have a majority over all other nationalities combined—the total number of Catholics given in the directory for that diocese is 70,000—the English speaking priests number 17 and the priests of other nationalities 80." The Union calculated that there were:

64,000 German speaking Catholics in Milwaukee and 91,000 English

21,000 German speaking Catholics in La Crosse and 39,000 English

29,000 German speaking Catholics in Green Bay and 34,500 English

Green Bay was more carefully analyzed than the others:

34,500	English	4,000	Hollanders
29,000	German	11,000	Poles
10,500	French	10,500	Bohemians
7,000	Walloon Belgian	1,500	Indians
2,000	Flemish Belgian		

But in 18 purely English parishes and in 16 predominantly English parishes there were 11 English pastors and 23 others.

Again, a few days before the installation the *Sentinel,* June 20, 1891, carried a two edged resolution of the Clerical Union

---

[23]One of the prime movers of this organization was Father Gmeiner, former editor of *Columbia* and professor at St. Francis Seminary. He left Milwaukee to join the diocese of St. Paul.

pledging loyalty to the pope and the Propaganda but denouncing Cahenslyism. It was the members "firm conviction that far greater numbers have been lost to the Church in consequence of the neglect of proper training and education in the language of the country than on account of the neglect of any foreign language." The document, which later alluded to the Monroe Doctrine, declared:

"The bishops of the Church in this country, who acknowledge the English language as their mother tongue have merited only honor, credit, and praise for the special sacrifices they have made to supply priests who might acceptably respond to the needs of all nationalities.

"Resolved that the rights of American Catholics in this country are paramount to all others; that their welfare should first be consulted; that their spiritual wants should first be supplied; that the rights of majorities should be never disregarded, and that in this, our own country, foreign customs, foreign ideas and foreign influences should not be imposed upon us, but rather that all Catholic immigrants to our beloved land should conform to American ways, learn the language of the country and aim to become good, loyal Americans as well as good Catholics."

Hardly had the excitement over Katzer's appointment and installation subsided when Cardinal Gibbons, normally elusive and smooth, astounded the nation in his sermon at the conferring of the pallium. If Katzer perchance thought himself remarkable for having defeated the Bennett law and outwitted the Republicans in spite of opposition from St. Paul, now he was publicly chastened by one in higher position. Said the cardinal:

"Woe to him, my brethren, who would destroy this blessed harmony that reigns among us! Woe to him who would sow tares of discord in the fair fields of the Church in America! Woe to him who would breed dissension among the leaders of Israel by introducing a spirit of nationalism into the camps of the Lord! Brothers we are, whatever may be our nationality, and brothers we shall remain—we will prove to our countrymen that the ties formed by grace and faith are stronger than flesh and blood—God and our country. This our watchword—Loyalty to God's church and to our country—this our religious and political faith."[24]

Granted that the proximate cause of this apostrophe lay in the current press reports concerning Cahenslyism, Gibbons could not have overlooked the fact that his action could embarrass the new archbishop and engender many unfounded suspicions. And it remains a fact that Gibbons' attention had been focused on Milwaukee years back when the suffragan bishops met to recommend a coadjutor for Archbishop Henni. Then Gibbons was expected to lend his weight to Spalding, and the cardinal was human enough to feel smitten first when Heiss defeated him and doubly so when Katzer triumphed ten years later. Notwithstanding the second rebuff, Archbishop Elder wanted Gibbons to block the appointment of a German successor to Green Bay. The cardinal, however, shrewdly suggested that those interested act separately without his leadership.

What Peter Paul Cahensly had started as simple charity a decade before Katzer's installation in Milwaukee had now been denounced as crafty intrigue. A new "ism" came into existence and Webster had a new term to accession. Even in congress it was berated as a vile political machination covered by the clean cloak of religion. Knowing that many shafts were aimed at him, Katzer wrote to Gibbons that he had nothing to do with the affairs of Cahensly. Katzer observed that he himself was an Austrian and that when he read the name Cahensly in the papers he did not know whether the man was a Swiss, German, or Slav. Irked by recent abuse he splurged at the end of his letter: "If I hold different opinions in the school question and with regard to societies is this a reason to belie me in a manner which is almost diabolical?"[25]

---

[24] James Cardinal Gibbons, *A Retrospect of Fifty Years* (Baltimore, 1916) vol. II, p. 151.

[25] *Catholic Historical Review*, Oct. 1946, p. 327. Colman Barry in his extensive research found nothing to incriminate Katzer.

Since the question of parochial schools was the key controversy in the archiepiscopal career of Katzer it deserves first consideration in an account of his life. Having been born before the middle of the century he knew only too well the old tradition of Josephism which had magnified the authority of the state to the detriment of the Church. Second, he had seen the development of the concordat which Austria-Hungary made with the Vatican in 1855. It was an epoch making event which favored the Church in the field of education, but, after Austria lost the war with Prussia in 1866, it was only a matter of time before the liberals succeeded in scrapping the concordat. Katzer and his circle saw Bishop Rudigier of Linz prosecuted and convicted for his pastoral on education and marriage; they studied the Prussian *Kulturkampf;* and they did not fail to notice similar events in Belgium. In all these controversies the rights of the Church respecting education were at stake. This information, much of it first hand, predetermined Katzer's thinking. Men of different backgrounds impatiently labeled it intransigent.

In pre-revolutionary America education had often been the work of the various Protestant churches, but during the first decades of the nineteenth century the increase of religious indifference, the multiplication of sects, and secularism in general slowly modified the American outlook. Fully aware of this change, the new leaders ultimately made it almost axiomatic that the state should educate and that the school program should omit religious training.

Simultaneously a few churchmen like Hughes fought for a share of public funds but most of them were content to build a rival school system. Basically all Catholics patronized it because of their religious convictions. Those who spoke a language other than English had a secondary motive, namely, the opportunity of having their children educated in the milieu of the home.[26] This assuredly stimulated generosity among recent immigrants, and when those outside the racial group observed the growth of these schools they became suspicious of and hostile to their foreign type

---

[26]The U. S. Supreme Court upheld this right in the case of Meyer vs. Nebraska, *U. S. Reports,* vol. 262, pp. 390-412.

of education. Prescinding from the views of non-Catholics, the cleavage was originally between Irish and German Catholics. Later the cleavage was between the Irish, German, and Slavic groups. This situation often existed in Wisconsin but Katzer was proud of his Catholic schools; the laymen knew what sacrifices they had made for them; and the council of Baltimore in 1884 again stressed Catholic education. In word as well as in deed Katzer took the decrees of the council on schools most seriously.[27]

According to the council, every parish that lacked a parochial school had to erect one within two years unless the bishop authorized a postponement. Since only 40% of the parishes had schools, the question arises: Did the fathers expect the number to increase to 90 or 95% by 1886? Or, did they employ this grave phraseology only to exalt an ideal that they knew was unattainable in many or most places? After eight years the percentage had risen only to 44% and after making allowance for the flood of immigration plus the natural increase of wealth in settled families, it appears that the legislation produced only negligible results.[28]

Aside from this digression into arithmetic there is no doubt that the Holy See and the various councils and synods consistently stressed the importance of parish schools. Against this background Archbishop Ireland in his bombastic manner eulogized the public school system in 1890 at a convention of the National Educational Association.[29]

Though the orator plainly pointed to its defects relative to religion, many Catholics squirmed at the general tone of his talk. They gasped when he, in line with his address, inaugurated a plan at Faribault which made the parochial school part of the

---

[27]Katzer was scrupulous when it came to rubrics. Old priests have told the writer of Katzer's scruples, and Rainer in his funeral sermon referred to his conscientiousness which at times bordered on scrupulousness.

[28]Theodore Roemer, *The Catholic Church in the United States* (St. Louis, 1950), pp. 291-292.

[29]John Ireland, *The Catholic Church and Modern Society* (New York, 1903), vol. I, p. 217.

public school system, with the proviso that religious instruction be given outside of school hours. This shocked those who had ardently defended parochial schools and Katzer became one of Ireland's most determined opponents in spite of the fact that several such compromise programs were operating in his own diocese.[30] Ironically enough, while Catholics were berating Ireland for sabotaging the parochial schools, others railed at him for undermining the public schools to the advantage of the Church.

Was Ireland running counter to the general attitude of the Church or was he merely developing a method of aiding parishes which could not possibly afford a school? Would this half-way measure make Catholics less generous in supporting their schools? Was the Faribault arrangement an exception to existing rules or the seed of a new system?

Two factions answered differently. Each tried to convert Rome to its viewpoint. In the end, the Vatican gave neither side a complete victory. When Cardinal Ledochowski announced the verdict *Tolerari potest* in the spring of 1892, some of the Ireland coterie trumpeted that this meant full approval. Obviously it didn't. And judging from the constant attitude of high churchmen the ideal of the Catholic school has never changed. Likewise, most non-Catholic Americans want no arrangements resembling the Faribault plan.

The controversy was intensified by a man whose interest in the problem was solely academic. Ireland made his speech in July 1890 and Rome passed judgment in spring of 1892, but in 1891 Dr. Thomas Bouquillon of the Catholic University published a pamphlet *Education To Whom Does It Belong?* His role assumed added significance because no Catholic of consequence had previously publicly defended the right of the state to educate.[31]

Today, because of totalitarianism, everyone sees the importance of limiting the rights of the state over children, but at that time

---

[30]Reilly, *op. cit.*, p. 255.
[31]*Ibid.*, p. 106.

the problem was especially acute in Wisconsin. Here the Bennett law was attacked precisely because it seemed to infringe on the rights of parents. Bouquillon's pamphlet de-emphasized their rights even if it did not violate Catholic principles. Needless to say, at the time few leaders limited themselves to such jejune remarks.

Even if Katzer escaped total defeat in Rome he felt floored. *Tolerari potest* was much too mild to suit his taste. In the public mind he lost prestige largely because his press agents were inferior to those of the opposition. Many Jesuits agreed with Katzer and consequently the opposition hailed the decision as a defeat of both the Germans and the Jesuits.

The pope, convinced of the gravity of the situation, sent Archbishop Satolli to the United States a few months after the decision *Tolerari potest* had been issued. Satolli delivered fourteen points to the hierarchy in regard to schools. These he presented at the meeting of metropolitans in New York. Both Katzer and Ireland were present. The points were so conciliatory that several archbishops recommended changes and the papal representative encountered spirited opposition to his ostensibly definitive message.

Zeininger probably fronted for Katzer when he commented that Satolli's speech was "objectionable" and that it was a "practical endorsement of the Faribault plan."[32] Besides expressing dissenting opinions, some questioned Satolli's right to settle the controversy. Katzer apparently was among them. As news reports flooded Rome, Pope Leo XIII retaliated by setting up the apostolic delegation. Henceforth an authoritative arbiter would live on this side of the sea. Satolli was the man. At first he leaned toward the Ireland-Gibbons faction, so for some years the conservative cause seemed lost.

The delegation was established in Washington in the shadow of the national capital. Temporarily Satolli lived at the new Catholic University. If Katzer, who was extremely pro-papal, was cool to Satolli's conciliatory message, he was equally cool to this edu-

---

[32]*Ibid.*, p. 217. *The Catholic Sentinel* (Chippewa Falls) Dec. 15, 1892.

cational venture of Gibbons, Ireland, and Spalding. He probably admired and applauded Father Schroeder, the well known professor of dogma whom the University dismissed in 1897. Twenty years later, at least, Margaret B. Downing in a diatribe[33] written under the emotional stress of World War I alleged without documentation that the "late Katzer of Milwaukee and Horstmann of Cleveland looked upon Schroeder as the Israelites of old on the prophets who had come to warn them of destruction."[34]

Katzer had been in the thick of another controversy in which he likewise advocated the more rigorous solution. It concerned secret societies. Toward the middle of the last century Catholic leaders in America began to be much concerned about all secret societies but, because it was hard to obtain information regarding their aims, condemnations were neither objective nor uniform. To obviate this the second plenary council of Baltimore, held in 1866, forbade anyone to make denunciations by name. Four years later the Holy See banned the Fenian Brotherhood while other groups of an Irish nature escaped condemnation even if they invited suspicion.

Despite their edifying rituals and kindly ideals, many secret societies ardently promoted the strictly secular public school. Bishop Baltes of Alton, for example, publicly referred to such a liaison, and the *American Catholic Quarterly Review* carried the remark: "The state has the right and duty to encourage good education but its right to educate is but a Masonic invention." In spring of 1884 Pope Leo XIII dealt with Masonry in an encyclical, *Humanum Genus*. Here he charged that a number of bodies "though differing in name, in ceremonial, in form and origin, are nevertheless so bound together by community of purpose and by the similarity of their main opinions, as to make them, in fact, one with the sect of the Freemasons, which is a kind of center whence they all go forth and whither they all return." The pope

---

[33] *Reedy's Mirror*, Aug. 13, 1917.

[34] Another rumor claimed that Katzer founded Preuss' *Review*. The editor denied the rumor. *Review*, July 30, 1903, p. 479. The *Review* rarely mentioned Katzer's name.

assailed them for propagating "the great error of this age—that a regard for religion should be held as an indifferent matter, and that all religions are alike." As for education the pontiff asserted: "With the greatest unanimity the sect of the Freemasons endeavors to take to itself the education of youth. . . . In the education and instruction of children they allow no share, either of teaching or of discipline, to the ministers of the Church; and in many places they have procured that the education of youth shall be exclusively in the hands of laymen, and that nothing which treats of the most important and most holy duties of men to God shall be introduced into the instructions on morals."[35]

Since the pope prescribed that sermons and pastoral letters instruct the laity concerning the artifices of secret societies, the third plenary council of Baltimore of necessity had to consider the matter. The assemblage concluded that no individual bishop should condemn a society. The archbishops of the country would serve as a judicial committee, and only a unanimous decision could take effect. Otherwise the matter had to be referred to the Holy See.[36]

After the council adjourned the question remained: What societies are forbidden? Archbishop Ireland thought the Odd Fellows and the Knights of Pythias could be tolerated but Catholics should be dissuaded from joining them. Gibbons, too, inclined toward leniency with the proviso that the members abide by any future action of the Church. Were Katzer's views not set forth in the preface to *Der Kampf der Gegenwart* (1873) one could conclude that he took sides in the quarrel primarily because he disliked the proponents of toleration. As a young priest he wrote: "A venal press, the omnipotence of capital and machinery

---

[35]Quoted from the Paulist Press Edition.
Katzer in a letter, Dec. 21, 1889, advised his flock: "The public school which is devoid of all religious and moral instruction is a Masonic invention and a most efficacious means, most shrewdly excogitated, to remove respect for religion and love of God from the hearts of the children."

[36]Fergus MacDonald, *The Catholic Church and the Secret Societies in the United States*, U. S. Catholic Historical Society, Monograph Series, vol. XXII.

on the one side, and the de-Christianization of the laborers on the other; a haughty, anti-religious science, the destructive principles of modern political theory, a false so-called liberalism which enslaves everything, *the dark, secret and anti-Christian activity of secret societies,* a false education, etc., have brought on the battle against all order, morality, and right, and have plunged Europe into the abyss of ruin."

At the first annual meeting of the archbishops in Boston in July of 1890 the consensus of opinion seemed to be that the Knights of Pythias and the Sons of Temperance were not formally condemned. Katzer eventually reported to Rome that the opinion gained wide credence that only the Masons were condemned. He wanted formal condemnation of these other groups and he maintained that a Roman decision given on August 21, 1850, to Archbishop Kenrick of Philadelphia, condemning the Odd Fellows and the Sons of Temperance was still in force. At the time Cardinal Fransoni had stressed that the Holy See objected to their secrecy even if they did not plot against church or state. Later documents made it possible to argue this point and unequivocal Katzer took his stand. In November of 1891 the archbishops met in St. Louis and Katzer took the floor to criticize last year's deliberations. These he had not attended because he was only bishop of Green Bay, and therefore his knowledge of them was not first hand.

Following the session at St. Louis he wrote a Latin letter to his clergy, dated February 14, 1892, stating that the archbishops did not want to change the Baltimore legislation regarding secret societies. The Masons and Carbonari are expressly excommunicated by name and "there can be no doubt that the Odd Fellows and Sons of Temperance are at least expressly forbidden by name." Adherents cannot be absolved until they have dropped their membership or seriously promised to do so. He admitted that there were various dangerous societies which the faithful should avoid. All societies admitting members of any or no faith and aping Masonic practices had better be shunned. Labor unions were appraised as licit in themselves but often dangerous to Catholics because they might transgress the limits of justice. Moreover, they tend in the direction of the forbidden societies and promote religious indifferentism by bringing together on intimate terms people of all faiths and of no faith. Christian burial was forbidden to Masons, Carbonari, Odd Fellows, and Sons of Temperance. Members of other groups could be buried from the Church provided the societies did not attend in a body, wear regalia, or perform any ceremonies excepting the strictly military honors of the G. A. R. Nothing was said about the Knights of Pythias whose doom was about to be sealed.

The same spring Katzer published an article in the *Catholic Citizen* and in the *American Ecclesiastical Review*. He defended the thesis that it was an error to believe that a Catholic may join any lodge other than the Masons. He distinguished clearly between prohibition and excommunication and went on to express a severe opinion on the Knights of Pythias. That November when the archbishops met for the third time they referred the matter to Rome. The Vatican quickly passed adverse judgment on the Odd Fellows, the Knights of Pythias, and the Sons of Temperance. Considerable time elapsed before the decision was promulgated because the American hierarchy had some discretionary power relative to making it known. The decision annoyed some and a few expected Gibbons to go to Rome and duplicate the victory he had won for the Knights of Labor.

The decision pleased Katzer but he did not rush into print with a special letter. He waited until he was ready to make his *ad limina*. Then he issued a pastoral letter, dated January 20, 1895, quoting the official condemnation of the three societies. He hoped that all would conform to it, and he reiterated that it is an error to believe that only those societies are forbidden which are designated by name. On the contrary, a society is forbidden if it violates the general rules on the subject.

On December 15, 1900, he again issued a long letter touching on a number of abuses, but a third of the document dealt with "doubtful societies", such as the Modern Woodman and the Maccabees. Granted that the priest should discourage joining them, what about absolution? No unqualified answer could be given, so Katzer repeated the general rules and concluded:

"Although I am personally convinced that the societies mentioned belong to those that are implicitly forbidden, I have no right to impose upon the penitent in the confessional my private opinion, but I must learn from the penitent through proper enquiry whether the society to which he belongs has the features of an implicitly forbidden society; and, likewise, I have no right as confessor to act in the case of one penitent in accordance with the confession of another.

"In these words I have simply expressed my private opinion on this difficult question, because I have been asked so often by priests, and because the practice of priests in this matter is so varied, some absolving all, others refusing absolution to all. I for my part believe that most of the societies, as they are constituted at present, founded by non-Catholics and containing members of every and of no religion, belong to the societies that are implicitly forbidden, and I admonish all the Reverend Fathers most urgently to keep the faithful from them."

By taking a definite stand on secret societies and maintaining it over the years Katzer alienated some people, but he attracted others who grew weary of "masterful inactivity" in the face of a burning question of the day. In Katzer they recognized an intrepid albeit severe man who made no effort to knit his admirers into an articulate following.[37]

The controversies about Cahensly, Catholic schools, and secret societies overwhelmed Katzer with publicity not only in Wiscon-

---

[37] Among the books which influenced Katzer was Abbé Henri Delassus, *L'Americanisme et la Conjuration Antichretienne*. Katzer gave this to William T. Doyle who had loaned the archbishop some Brownsonia. Doyle to Henry Brownson, Milwaukee, Oct. 10, 1899. In ND archives. In the same archives is a letter of Katzer to Henry F. Brownson, Green Bay, July 11, 1890, ordering Brownson's pamphlet *The Religion of Ancient Craft Masonry*. He said: "It is a vindication of a speech of mine for which I was censured by such who claim that American Masonry is innocent." He wished for similar pamphlets on the Odd Fellows which was blunt Masonry, only more dangerous because some claim membership is not forbidden.

sin but in many states. Within the diocese itself very little happened during the first two years of his administration and in 1893 the national depression began to cramp churchmen as well as business men. However, in 1891 the archbishop celebrated the silver jubilee of his ordination without fanfare in the parish at Hartford where he had offered his first Mass and about the same time the diocese bought a residence[38] for him at a cost of $62,000. The following February he consecrated Bishop Schwebach[39] for the diocese of La Crosse and that same year he presided over a synod at the seminary.

As stated above, Katzer made his *ad limina* in 1895. Besides publishing the Roman decision on secret societies he used the occasion to preach with his pen on the virtue of obedience. Seven years earlier, when he was bishop of Green Bay, the pope had asked whether his people and priests were obedient. Anticipating a similar query he rejoiced that he could again answer affirmatively —especially in regard to the school laws of Baltimore. Mixed in with much praise was some blame. "Unfortunately," he observed, "we cannot say that everywhere, where it would be possible, a Catholic school exists, but in several of those places the priests and people have taken steps which allow us to hope confidently that soon there, and finally in all places where possible, next to the church a nursery of our holy faith will arise for the youth. . . . A parish which has no Catholic school is half a thing, and in a parish whose members do not show a warm interest in a parochial school, Catholic life is lacking. . . . A child which does not attend a Catholic school is deprived of the means of being adequately instructed and reared in its holy religion. Sunday School or Holy Communion instructions cannot supply for this deficiency,

---

[38] This property served to test the Wisconsin laws on taxation and incorporation. Patrick J. Dignan, *A History of the Legal Incorporation of Catholic Church Property in the United States (1784-1932)* (New York, 1935), pp. 235-236.

[39] After Gibbons' sermon at the pallium ceremony Ireland probably expected that an English speaking bishop would be appointed to La Crosse. Barry, *op cit.*, p. 164. Katzer consecrated Bishop Eis for Marquette in 1899.

and only in very rare cases is home training and instruction such that the Catholic school can be dispensed with."

As for Bouquillon's thesis and the philosophy underlying the Bennett law he observed: "Without doubt the state has the right to demand of parents that they rear their children so that they become useful, upright, patriotic citizens, ready to defend their fatherland not only with proper phrases but also with their property and their blood."

After bidding farewell to his flock Katzer, accompanied by Zeininger, went to New York where he spent several days with the Capuchins before sailing. He arrived at Naples on February 16. Five days later he had his audience with Leo XIII. Next he visited Cardinals Steinhuber, Parocchi, and Rampolla, and by March 1 he was ready to leave Rome for Alexandria. Bad weather plagued him and his being a poor horseman restricted his activity still more. From the Holy Land he went to Austria for a prolonged stay. Here, besides returning to his alma mater at Freinberg, he visited several families which had furnished priests for the Milwaukee archdiocese. This time his stay at Linz was unusually pleasant because his old friend and schoolmate, Doppelbauer, was the new bishop. Both churchmen, for example, went together to Ebensee and, after the bishop left, Katzer and Father Hodnett remained to participate in the meeting of a Catholic labor union. The climax of his visit came when Doppelbauer presented him in front of the cathedral to Emperor Francis Joseph who happened to be making an official visit that year.

While at Linz, Father Gulski of Milwaukee visited him and Archbishop Zardetti of Bucharest stopped there while en route to Switzerland. Besides enjoying such calls in Austria, Katzer dropped in to chat with Dr. Lieber at Camberg. At the Notre Dame convent in Munich he met Bishop Foley of Detroit and Cardinal Gibbons who planned to go to Woerishofen to consult Monsignor Kneipp, the expert in hydrotherapy. From southeastern Europe Katzer made his way via Cologne to Rotterdam whence he sailed for America on September 25 aboard the *S. S. Veendam*. Upon his arrival in Milwaukee the usual Victorian formalities were observed; ten thousand people lined the streets to greet him; and Dean McGinnity presented him with a purse of $2,100.[40]

During his stay in Rome Katzer had visited the newly organized Sisters of the Divine Savior and suggested that some come to Milwaukee to nurse the sick in their homes. Although Katzer did not return until October, several sisters arrived in July. Using Milwaukee as their headquarters the community expanded its program and on March 8, 1896, Katzer offered the first order of the Divine Savior the establishment at St. Nazianz to perpetuate at least in a modified way the ideals of Father Oschwald which were then threatened with extinction. Father Jordan came personally to inspect the place and appraise its possibilities. The Salvatorians accepted, and St. Nazianz promptly attained fame for its Catholic press, its clerical education, and its missionary activity.[41]

Meanwhile the United States prepared to elect a president. Cleveland's second term was up and, since he had been blamed for the panic of 1893, the Democrats could scarcely anticipate victory. Widespread agitation for social, if not socialistic, reform had recently culminated in the Populist party, but in 1896 the Populists cast their lot with the Democrats. In the course of the campaign many clergymen[42] of different faiths expressed their

---

[40] *Columbia* carried a series of articles written by Zeininger describing the journey.

During the archbishop's absence the bishops of the province issued a letter commemorating the fact that twenty-five years had elapsed since Italy despoiled the Holy Father of his temporal sovereignty.

[41] Father Jordan knew Bishop Doppelbauer from the time of the latter's residence in Rome. The Salvatorians opened several places in Austria-Hungary. Oschwald had come to Wisconsin in 1854 with 113 men and women to establish a Catholic lay community in the wilderness. Katzer said in his letter that the community at the time had 1,500 acres and $40,000 capital. Pancratius Pfeiffer, *Father Francis Mary of the Cross Jordan Founder and First Superior General of the Society of the Divine Savior*, tr. by Winfrid Herbst (St. Nazianz, 1936), pp. 447, 385; Heming, *op. cit.*, pp. 941-942.

[42] *The World*, New York, Oct. 25, 1896, carried a letter from Archbishop Ireland referring to the "spirit of socialism" and "the war of the proletariat against the property-holder."

opinions on the questions of the day which involved religious principles and shortly before the election Katzer followed suit.

The press quite generally reported an interview with Zeininger[43] who declared that Katzer endorsed his views. The former could not find "a single point in favor of the free coinage of silver". He saw "only social revolution following its adoption". Bryan had to be defeated by a large vote. Free silver would benefit neither the laborer nor the debtor. Hard times have other causes than the monetary system. Zeininger and his superior suggested that the depression resulted from the neglect of foreign trade, and, in view of the fact that the United States produced more than it could consume, they recommended trading with Mexico and South America. To the argument that silver would force prices up they rebutted that "wages are always the last to rise, and they rise the shortest distance". Silver was simply too cheap a metal to be used for currency. In their opinion it would be better to issue greenbacks than to authorize the free coinage of silver in the proportion of 16 to 1 because the silver barons would derive the most benefit from such a program.

By making these views public Katzer aligned himself with McKinley[44] who carried Wisconsin and the industrial east. Bryan carried the south and west but lost by ninety-five electoral votes. Katzer had no appreciable influence on the vote but in the public eye he was curiously aligned with Archbishop Ireland who also rejected bimetallism. For Wisconsin politics the election marks a turning point because then the Socialists broke with the Populists to launch their own Social Democratic Party. In its infancy it failed to command Katzer's attention but in its prime it caused his successor a great deal of uneasiness.

---

[43]*Catholic Citizen*, Oct. 17, 1896, reported that Zeininger's pamphlet had been translated into six languages.

On another occasion Zeininger spoke for Katzer when he denied that the latter had protested to Rome against the reinstatement of Dr. McGlynn.

[44]Following the president's assassination Katzer sang a pontifical Mass *Pro pace* in the cathedral. He ordered all pastors to arrange similar services in their churches.

Two years after the election Katzer eulogized Leo XIII at the forty-third convention of the Central Verein which met in his see city. The speech found its way into the convention report and thereby escaped oblivion. The epideictic address drew its inspiration from the Holy Father's diamond sacerdotal jubilee. However, while Katzer mentioned *Rerum Novarum* specifically he gave no evidence of a profound appreciation of the social problem despite the fact that the widespread misery of the early nineties had elicited a plethora of economic and political proposals. Not all of them were reprehensible. But, being conservative in other matters, he looked askance at all programs which had been rightly or wrongly labeled radical. Harassed by a fixed idea he used the occasion to hark back to the school controversy. Religion, according to him, must penetrate all branches of learning and "Leo's conviction and Leo's teaching is that the rules of the council of Baltimore remain in force. The Catholic school is the school for Catholics."

Earlier that year when the war with Spain broke out Katzer kept perfectly silent. By contrast many of his peers were conspicuous for their vehement patriotism.[45] They enjoyed applauding and being applauded. Yet there was something unseemly in their protestations of loyalty. True, they tried to allay the perennial suspicions which the A. P. A. had recently rejuvenated, but they also flirted with the black legend common to the Anglo-Saxon and Protestant tradition. In Catholic circles of Europe, at least, Spain traditionally enjoyed prestige and the ecclesiastical angles of this war may have further impelled Leo XIII to speak on Americanism.

To say precisely what this term includes is impossible because it applies to tendencies rather than facts or declarations. It sums up all attempts to color Catholic teaching so as to make it more attractive to Protestant Americans and Catholics infatuated with ideas of progress and liberalism. In some instances it might mean minimizing the Church's position on public schools and secret societies; in others it might mean co-operating with inter-faith con-

---

[45] B. J. Blied, *Four Essays* (Milwaukee, 1949), p. 47 ff.

ferences or speaking in Protestant churches; in others it might mean extolling the active life of the parish priest to the detriment of the monastic life; or it might refer to the opinion that the Holy Ghost guides individuals more in this era than He did in other eras, and even some racial theories concerning the qualities of North-Europeans in contrast to South-Europeans fall within the ambit of the term.

Most churchmen on this side of the sea blandly denied that such a congeries of errors ever existed. However, it seems that questionable tendencies did exist. And it is possible for men of high ideals and noble intentions to be misled. The metropolitan of Milwaukee and his suffragans, all of whom shied away from playing the part of patriot-prelates, wrote to the Holy Father[46]:

"We received the apostolic letter of Your Holiness on the errors called by the name of Americanism with all the more joy and gratitude because the decision of the infallible See appeared to us very opportune.

"That we have thus far omitted to manifest to Your Holiness the sentiments of our hearts is certainly not due to any want of piety toward our Father, nor to negligence in a matter of gravest importance; but we thought that no answer was expected from those who have abhorred these errors from the very beginning of the controversy and that it was self evident that dutiful sons would listen to and embrace gladly and thankfully the admonitions of a most loving Father.

"Since, however, some people seem to abuse our silence and omission, and to interpret them in an evil manner and according to their own desires, we consider it our duty no longer to delay our response, but to express to Your Holiness our very great and most profound gratitude for the truly Apostolical letter, in which errors that are not foreign to some people in this country, are so firmly, though gently repressed; the infallible magisterium of the Church and her Supreme Chief have thereby again been strengthened, the traditions of the Church profitably sustained and defined, the

---

[46]*The Review*, July 27, 1899, p. 145.

danger of innovation happily warded off, and the faithful confirmed in the pure and entire ancestral faith.

"Without any hesitation or reservation of mind, and without any restriction whatsoever, we therefore declare unanimously that we accept with filial obedience and with fullest assent the Apostolic Letter on the errors of Americanism, and that we have thus accepted it most religiously from the beginning.

"While congratulating Your Holiness with all our hearts upon the fatherly and kind indulgence wherewith you have, while condemning the errors, recalled the erring to the way of right thinking, we cannot, however, help expressing our pain and just indignation over the fact that not a few have been found among our countrymen, and so many especially among the Catholic newspaper editors, who indeed affirmed that they reprobated and rejected the aforesaid errors, but did not hesitate to proclaim again and again, in Jansenistic fashion, that there was hardly any American who had held them and that the Holy See, deceived by false reports, had beaten the air and chased after a shadow, to use a popular expression.

"It can escape no loyal Catholic how injurious to the infallible See and how alien to the orthodox faith such conduct is, since those erroneous opinions have most assuredly and evidently been proclaimed among us orally and in writing, though perhaps not always so openly; and no true Catholic can deny that the magisterium of the Church extends not only to the revealed truths, but also to facts connected with dogma, and that it appertains to this teaching office to judge infallibly of the objective sense of any doctrine and the existence of false opinions.

"We moreover deplore vehemently the mode of speaking and writing of some, even Catholics, by which they traduce those who have admitted the existence of the errors of Americanism among us and signified to Your Holiness their assent and gratitude for your Apostolic Letter,—as rather unfriendly to their country and its institutions; although it must be manifest to every sane and truth-loving man that the Apostolic letter contains not a word of censure for the American Republic, not for our laws and institutions, nor finally for our peculiar customs and national endowments, but solely for the opinions brought in and uttered by some —by the condemnation of which most assuredly no disgrace nor injury nor brand has been stamped either upon the American Republic and its citizens or upon the Catholics of America.

"Against these, who drag a matter that appertains solely to Catholic doctrine and to the Church, into civil affairs, we therefore declare solemnly that we consider the Apostolic letter on the errors of Americanism opportune, and that we joyfully accept and embrace it; that we reprobate the condemned errors according to the mind of the Holy See, and that we remain attached with no less piety and loving devotion to our fatherland America and the welfare and prosperity of its citizens and the Republic.

"This it is which the ordinaries of the province of Milwaukee in the United States of America desired to write to Your Holiness.

"Prostrated at the feet of Your Holiness, we humbly beg the Apostolic benediction for ourselves and the faithful people committed to our care, offering thee the wishes of our filial love and obedience. Milwaukee, Pentecost Sunday, 1899."

FREDERICK XAV. KATZER,	SEBASTIAN G. MESSMER,
Archbishop of Milwaukee	Bishop of Green Bay
JAMES SCHWEBACH,	FREDERICK EIS,
Bishop of La Crosse	Administrator of Marquette

That autumn, when the archbishops met in Baltimore, Katzer was absent but not forgotten. Archbishop Riordan rose to call attention to his letter which he considered of utmost importance because it raised the charge of heresy. Archbishop Kain proposed that some kind of protest be made against the Milwaukee letter. Then Archbishop Ireland moved that all bishops in America be asked: 1) whether these errors exist in their dioceses or in other parts of the country, and 2) if so, they should specify where and by whom they are held. Archbishop Corrigan, a fairly intimate friend of Katzer, countered that such action would be disrespectful to the Holy Father. At voting time the group was equally divided. Finally, Cardinal Gibbons voted nay and ended the matter.

Time passed and the new century dawned but it brought no noteworthy changes to the Church of Wisconsin.[47] However, on January 24, 1902, the archbishop wrote a long letter to his flock announcing his intention of going to Rome. Accordingly, he wished that his people would contribute generously to the Peter's Pence. That year Pope Leo XIII marked the silver jubilee of his election to the see of Peter. Since the pope was especially concerned about repairing the archbasilica of the Most Holy Redeemer, priests everywhere were expected to contribute the equivalent of one Mass stipend toward this work. The laity were to be edified with addresses and celebrations in honor of the Holy Father, whereas ladies' organizations and religious communities were to make, gather, and exhibit church goods. This would ultimately find its way to poor mission churches. Katzer spoke of the Indian schools and, after praising the generosity of the laboring class, he queried whether wealthy Catholics did as much for the honor of God as many non-Catholics did according to their convictions. Miss Catherine Drexel, he recalled, not only gave her life to the Indians but pledged $70,000 annually to the Indian schools. However, much more would be needed to preserve the faith which the early missionaries had planted in the aborigines. He laconically observed that the diocese had for years contributed nothing to the Catholic University and that Cardinal Gibbons had asked him to banish this ennui from his flock. He commended the House of the Good Shepherd which was in financial distress and, since this was to be his only letter for a whole year, he closed by outlining the financial obligations of parishes during the year.

For two years before this letter appeared the archbishop had been suffering from a liver ailment. After issuing the letter he

---

[47] In a circular of Dec. 15, 1900, Katzer discussed St. Michael's Priest Fund. A decree of the bishop and a statute of the synod of 1892 compelled every priest to contribute to the support of indigent priests. Lately it was proposed to form a society paying $600 yearly to all retired priests regardless of their financial condition. Katzer expressed the opinion that building a home for retired priests would not satisfy men who had previously enjoyed considerable liberty and authority. His opinion was that he could not *compel* priests to support an organization not limited to helping indigent priests. The letter discussed the project without settling anything.

made his last will and testament giving wide powers to Bishop Schwebach. Believing all to be in readiness for any emergency, he closed his desk and set out on his journey with Father Abbelen as a traveling companion.

In Europe Katzer, Abbelen, and Doppelbauer visited the ever fascinating scenes of the archbishop's youth. If the journey seemed to rejuvenate him, this was more apparent than real. In March of 1903 he entered St. Agnes Hospital, Fond du Lac, as a patient. Though he left the hospital only during Holy Week, he was not uninterruptedly in bed. Nor did he lay aside his administrative duties. In May he signed the papers of incorporation for the archdiocese, not in preparation for death but to put the legal status of the archdiocese in proper order. About the same time he published a booklet standardizing instruction as well as textbooks.[48] The preliminary work, of course, had been done by a committee of clergymen who had the difficult task of limiting local authority and aligning the exclusively English schools with the others.

None the less the archbishop's strength waned steadily. He had been a short, stocky man but at the time of his death he weighed only 110 pounds. Yet when Archbishop Falconio, the apostolic delegate, visited him three weeks before he died he was still able to go to the dining room. A little over a week before his death Father Kersten administered Extreme Unction. He died peacefully after exclaiming "Jesus, Mary, Joseph". The archbishop of Milwaukee passed away at the age of fifty-nine on July 20, 1903, the same day that Leo XIII died.[49] The apostolic delegate could not attend the obsequies because of the memorial services for the Holy Father in the east. In St. John's Cathedral, Milwaukee, Bishop Schwebach offered the funeral Mass, Archbishop Hennessy preached in English, and Father Rainer, a fellow Austrian, said farewell in German. Interment was in the idyllic

---

[48]*Northwestern Chronicle*, May 9, 1903; June 27, 1903.

[49]When Katzer was told about the death of the pope he was still sufficiently alert to comment on his greatness.

seminary cemetery where he lies between his parents. The *Northwestern Chronicle* commented that Katzer had overcome racial tension and added: "He might sometimes be impulsive; he was always just. He might sometimes be brusque; he was always kind."[50]

By contrast, Archbishop Ireland outlived Katzer by fifteen years. The former lived to see his beloved France allied with the United States fighting against Germany and Austria. Then, too, he had the opportunity of creating a good impression for himself after domestic hostilities had somewhat subsided. Of course, he had to endure the humiliation of not becoming a cardinal despite the widely publicized efforts of his influential friends. And judged from the vantage point of today, it seems certain that Ireland's method of handling current problems failed to become the *modus vivendi* of the Church in America. For better or for worse, the responsibility for this rests partly upon his neighbor, the third archbishop of Milwaukee.

---

[50]*Ibid.*, July 25, 1903. Rev. J. H. Hellstern of Barton bolted at his brusqueness. In 1896 Katzer made the statement that he was mentally deranged. A libel suit followed that reached the state supreme court. *Wisconsin Reports*, vol. 103, p. 391.

III

SEBASTIAN MESSMER

When Bishop Bayley came to the diocese of Newark as its first bishop, he came to a state that could boast of Princeton and Rutgers, but all New Jersey had no Catholic college. He himself belonged to the cultured aristocracy and to the alumni of Amherst. Believing that class consciousness was strong in America, Bayley concluded that the best way to impress Protestants was to elevate the social status of Catholics.

A year after his arrival he bought land for Seton Hall. This he entrusted to Father McQuaid, later the bishop of Rochester. The latter's friend, Michael Corrigan, later archbishop of New York, also presided over Seton Hall in its early years. Like many schools of this period Seton Hall was a combination seminary and college. The latter part predominated.

To this college-seminary youthful Father Messmer came one autumn day in 1871. Born on August 29, 1847, in the small Swiss village of Goldach, not far from Lake Constance, at baptism he received the name of his father, Sebastian. The latter, a farmer and innkeeper, had managed to advance himself financially and intellectually without the benefit of formal higher education, and, besides enjoying local prestige, he represented his district in the General Assembly. In all, he and his wife, née Rosa Baumgartner, had five children. The first of them was Sebastian.

After attending the village school he spent three years at the *Realschule* in Rorschach. Here he met Otto Zardetti,[1] a native of that place, who became a lifelong friend. From 1861 to 1866 he studied at St. George College near St. Gall, and upon finishing

---

[1] Zardetti left Switzerland in 1881. He taught at St. Francis Seminary and in 1887 became vicar-general of Bishop Marty. He became successively bishop of St. Cloud, archbishop of Bucharest, and a canon of St. Maria Maggiore in Rome. He died in 1902.

his classical studies he immersed himself in philosophy and theology for five years at the University of Innsbruck. For the stripling in his soutane they were years of quiet assimilation; for the world they were hectic and highly consequential.

In the United States the north and south were recuperating—unevenly, of course,—from the Civil War. In Europe, Protestant Prussia defeated Catholic Austria. Four years later France, traditionally a Catholic country, fell victim to Prussia. With France engaged on her northern boundary, Italy could easily annex Rome. Forthwith Pope Pius IX became "the prisoner of the Vatican". But while the outlook for Europe grew gloomier Messmer dreamed more and more of the United States. Young in years and youthful in ideals, this nation was a topic of general conversation. Messmer's enthusiasm swept away all barriers when Bishop Bayley arrived in Austria to recruit priests for New Jersey.

Back in 1862 Messmer had served Mass for Bishop Henni[2] when the latter visited his fatherland seeking donations while en route to Rome to attend the canonization of the Japanese martyrs. Now he had a chance to imitate that heroic Swiss prelate by volunteering for the American missions. The student, however, was not gambling with hardships because he was to live in the east where Bayley promised to make him a professor of theology. On July 23, 1871, Bishop Zuber, O.F.M.Cap., ordained Messmer at Innsbruck and a week later the young priest offered his first Mass at Goldach. Father Zardetti, just twenty-four years old, preached the sermon. On October 4 Messmer docked in New York, and without delay he mounted the rostrum in New Jersey where he spent eighteen years teaching Sacred Scripture, Canon Law, and sundry other branches.

Soon the professor became familiar with Wisconsin. His younger brother, Joseph, who had given up the "Rietli", which he inherited from his father, came to the United States to enter

---

[2]*Gedenkblaetter auf das Goldene Priesterjubilaeum des Hochw. Herrn Bonaventura Frey, O. M. Cap.* (New York, 1904), p. 10. Messmer himself edited this pamphlet and contributed the foreword.

the religious life. In 1875 the professor introduced him to the Capuchins who had assumed some obligations in New York City and before long Joseph went to Mt. Calvary, near Fond du Lac, where two secular Swiss priests had established the order in 1856. After his ordination Father Gabriel, as he came to be known, exercised his ministry in Milwaukee. Here he stayed seven years being, as it were, the precursor of his more famous brother.[3]

While Joseph familiarized himself with the environs of Lake Winnebago, Sebastian built up a solid reputation as a professor and author in New Jersey. Besides reading and teaching Canon Law, he acquired considerable practical information. In 1883 he published *Praxis Synodalis* for the provincial council of New York. Though little more than a pamphlet based upon Gavantus, it saw more than one edition and apparently filled a need. Prior to the third plenary council of Baltimore he was appointed to the board of theologians which worked on the agenda; during the council he served as a secretary; and later he and O'Connell edited its conclusions.

In recognition of his service to the council Pope Leo XIII conferred upon him the title Doctor of Divinity. Now that some prestige supplemented his ability, he proceeded to publish an English translation of Father Droste's German treatise, *Canonical Procedure in Disciplinary and Criminal Cases of Clerics. A Systematic Commentary on the "Instructio S. C. Epp. et Reg., 1880"*. A priest in Covington, however, had done the actual translating. Messmer merely adapted it to American conditions and in the preface he expressed his preference for English rather than Latin terminology.

All along Messmer kept in touch with pastoral work. He never became a specialist. Being a German speaking Swiss, he readily found his way to the large German element in the Newark diocese. Prominent among its leaders was Father Prieth, a Tyrolese who had been pastor of St. Peter's in Newark since 1855. Mess-

---

[3]Celestine N. Bittle, *A Romance of Lady Poverty; the History of the Province of St. Joseph of the Capuchin Order in the United States* (Milwaukee, 1933), p. 388 ff.

mer went to this church every week to help with pastoral chores and when Prieth died he succeeded him for a year. Besides working in this large parish he was pastor of St. Leo's in Irvington for two and a half years. This parish sprang up in the neighborhood of Seton Hall and temporarily the college chapel served as the parish church. Later he cared for St. Venantius Church in Orange which likewise was a new parish. Next he became less a pastor and more a professor.

In 1889 Bishop Keane, the rector of the Catholic University, traveled through Europe trying to assemble a capable faculty for his school. He had hoped to secure a Roman scholar as professor of Canon Law but, while visiting in the eternal city, he was urged to take Messmer for that post. When the latter received Keane's cablegram he consulted two antipodal characters: Cardinal Gibbons and Archbishop Corrigan. To the latter he confided that the position would suit his taste. Both agreed that Messmer would be an excellent man, so he cabled his acceptance.[4] That August Messmer started out on his first trip back to the scenes of his youth. His destination was Rome where he spent eight months at the Apollinaris College studying Canon Law. The following June he received the degree, Doctor of Canon Law, and set out for Washington.

No sooner had the University opened its doors when it became the hub of bitter controversies which crystallized Catholic thought and caused priests and people to gravitate toward different poles. The press, which was generous with space, bracketed professors as conservative or liberal, and as the Germans generally belonged to the former group Messmer shared their lot. Yet he was diplomatic enough not to become polemical when he risked reviewing the current controversial literature in the newly founded *American Ecclesiastical Review*.[5]

---

[4] Patrick Henry Ahern, *The Catholic University of America 1887-1896 The Rectorship of John J. Keane* (Washington, 1948), pp. 23-24.

[5] *American Ecclesiastical Review*, February, 1892, pp. 104-119; April, 1892, pp. 279-298.

The editor, Father Heuser, taught Sacred Scripture in St. Charles Seminary in Philadelphia and took a liking to Messmer. Writing to him in 1891 Messmer expressed annoyance at the attack which Archbishop Ireland's paper, *The Northwestern Chronicle,* had made on himself for upholding clerical unions. If Ireland charged that they fostered nationalism, Messmer branded that nonsensical. Heuser asked for an article on the subject but since Keane disliked the controversy Messmer declined the invitation.[6] The next year Messmer confided to the editor that many German papers had blindly attacked Bouquillon, his fellow professor, and hence had made rash statements. On the other hand, it was "simply an insult" to allege that recent laws enraged the Germans merely because they would have to teach English in their parochial schools. The real cause for alarm was fear lest their schools be turned into state schools.[7] Messmer praised Heuser for keeping abreast of the times and yet remaining sufficiently conservative to save the Church from the disastrous consequences of the thinking which characterized the end of the century. At that time even many clergymen knew "very little, if anything at all, of the true principles determining the extent of liberty in theological matters."[8]

Besides being harassed by household hostilities with far flung implications, the professors at Washington were deflated by a lack of students. In the third year of the University's existence, for example, only 33 students, most of whom were not priests, attended the lectures of the faculty of theology—and that in a school which claimed to serve the entire nation and feature graduate work.[9]

After Messmer had been teaching slightly more than a year Archbishop Katzer informed him that he had been appointed

---

[6]Colman Barry, *The Catholic Church and German Americans* (Milwaukee, 1953), p. 127.

[7]*Ibid.,* p. 192.

[8]*Ibid.,* p. 189.

[9]Ahern, *op. cit.,* p. 50.

bishop of Green Bay. Far from being elated he asked O'Connell, the rector of the American College in Rome, to avert his appointment. To him it was imprudent to remove men from the University after they had been trained for classroom work. Believing it a simple matter to find a bishop for Green Bay, he begged both Gibbons and Corrigan to defeat his promotion. Bishop Keane apparently tried to keep him, but he was later represented as having machinated to ease him out of the university. When Keane inquired about this gossip, Messmer replied affably but made unpleasant references to the faculty. Throughout life he held to the opinion that his colleagues had plotted to get him out of Washington. Precisely at the moment when the University was trying to replace Messmer, Archbishop Ireland lectured Keane: "You must educate your professors and then hold on to them—making bishops only of those who are not worth keeping as professors."[10] Besides lamenting the empty rostrum, Ireland rued the fact that a German-American succeeded Katzer in Green Bay. La Crosse, which became vacant almost simultaneously, also failed to go to an English speaking bishop.[11]

Messmer received the news of his appointment late in 1891, but he deferred his consecration until the fourth Sunday of the following Lent. For his consecrator Messmer selected Otto Zardetti, a friend of student days who had followed him to America. The latter had served successively as professor in St. Francis Seminary, as vicar general of Bishop Marty in the Dakotas, and as bishop of St. Cloud, Minnesota. When Messmer chose a place to be consecrated he again looked backward. He had served St. Peter's parish, Newark, and there he wanted to be consecrated. The strains of Singenberger's music heralded the event and Bishop McQuaid of Rochester, long connected with Seton Hall and the most obstreperous opponent of the Catholic University, preached the sermon. Bishop Keane of the University and Bishop Wigger, formerly of Seton Hall, were the co-consecrators. Cardinal Gib-

---

[10] *Ibid.*, pp. 50-51, 159.
[11] Barry, *op. cit.*, p. 164.

bons donated the episcopal ring to the new bishop, and Archbishop Corrigan, a fellow Seton Hall man, spoke at the dinner following the consecration.

Messmer traveled to his see via Milwaukee. Here he called on Archbishop Katzer and took time to visit the seminary. When the train reached Chilton on Thursday afternoon at 5:30 it stopped for fifteen minutes to allow the new bishop to alight and shake hands with some of the fifteen hundred people who had gathered at the southern boundary of his diocese to welcome him. Delegates had come from Green Bay and Appleton to escort him and a band added color to the event. More formalities were the order of the day in Green Bay but he found time to compose a pastoral letter which he issued the following Sunday, Palm Sunday. After Easter he began exploring the diocese making his first official visit to St. Patrick's Church in Fort Howard where he hastened to assure his hearers that a bishop is not appointed to any one nationality.

He found his see in fair condition[12] considering that it was just twenty-four years old. Embracing 120,000 faithful and counting over 100 priests it was not small even though it lay far from the urbane Atlantic seaboard where Messmer had lived for twenty-one years. On the other hand, a climate of opinion prevailed that galled him. The prohibition movement was gaining momentum, bombastic patriotism reverberated in many auditoriums, Archbishop Ireland's compromise school program cropped up often in the Green Bay *State Gazette,* and the word "Cahenslyism" struck terror into some and stoked the fire of fury in others. Even the office he held was rivaled by an adventurer who had just contrived to have himself consecrated a bishop.

First of all Messmer had to cope with this "Archbishop Vilatte". A Parisian by birth, he had been ordained an "Old Catholic" priest in Switzerland and later he secured schismatic consecration in Ceylon. As an appendage of the Episcopalian

---

[12] For the aid which Messmer received from the Ludwig Mission Society see Theodore Roemer, "Munich and Green Bay", *Salesianum,* April, 1940, p. 80.

diocese of Fond du Lac he tried to proselyte the Belgians living northeast of Green Bay, but later he tried to build up a following among disaffected Poles throughout the nation. To offset the influence of the affable Vilatte, Messmer invited Premonstratensians from Holland to take over the churches in that area. The first of the group arrived in 1893. Besides undoing his misdeeds they methodically bolstered up the faith of many and eventually they enriched the diocese with St. Norbert's College. The affair brought Messmer and Satolli, the apostolic delegate, into close contact because Vilatte, alternately penitent and impenitent, tried to play the two against each other for his own profit.[13]

In 1892 Messmer began raising funds for an orphanage and he also built St. Aloysius Institute at Sevastopol, a crossroads in the cherry country north of Sturgeon Bay. Since he paid for the Institute personally and blessed it on November 29 of that same year it probably absorbed the gifts he received at his consecration. St. Aloysius accommodated forty boarders who received instruction from the sisters in German, English, or French as the needs of each case demanded. It is interesting to note that Messmer ultimately entrusted this establishment to a fellow Swiss, Father Constantine Ulrich, a classmate at Innsbruck, who volunteered to come to America the same time that the bishop agreed to go to New Jersey. Thanks to this school, parents living more or less in isolation could have their children prepared for the sacraments at little cost.[14]

By the end of 1892 newspaper reports about Satolli's decision on parochial schools and about Cahenslyism had exhausted Messmer's patience. He wrote to the Green Bay *State Gazette* rebutting an interview with Archbishop Ireland which had appeared under the headline "The Controversy Settled". Said Messmer in the issue of January 4, 1893:

---

[13]Joseph Marx and B. J. Blied, "Joseph Réné Vilatte," *Salesianum*, Jan., April, July, 1942.

[14]Harry H. Heming, *The Catholic Church in Wisconsin* (Milwaukee, 1898), pp. 987-988, 728-729. *Rorschacher Zeitung*, Jan. 27, 1925.

"The controversy, that is, the question concerning the position of the Catholic Church in America in regard to Catholic education and the necessity of Catholic schools for Catholic children is settled indeed. It had been finally settled eight years ago, not by Mgr. Satolli or the archbishops, but by the third plenary council of Baltimore. The resolutions passed by the archbishops in New York are a new endorsement of the rule laid down by that council. Mgr. Satolli's address also, as published later in pamphlet form, is another endorsement of the Baltimore decree, so much so that one of our brightest and we trust leading Catholic weeklies, *The New World,* Chicago, openly declares that 'the much-talked-of address of Archbishop Satolli sets forth nothing new or startling in regard to Catholic education and the relation of Church and State. It will be seen, indeed, that every practical suggestion made by him had been already anticipated by the bishops of this country and put into active and actual application.' (Allow me to say here that the fifth section of Archbishop Satolli's essay is a *garbled* quotation from the Baltimore council and makes the reader understand the very contrary from what the council did say. Decree 198, forbidding bishop or priest to exclude from the sacraments as unworthy those parents who send their children to public schools, is *restricted* to such cases where the parents have for good reason obtained the necessary permission from their own bishop. But in law, as you know, the exception proves the rule.) So far, then, the controversy is settled.

"But the school question which 'for more than a year agitated the church in America' is not settled and remains today where it was before the New York conference for the simple reason that the proposed 'settlement' was not accepted by the archbishops. From the official report of the conference (printed for *private* circulation among the bishops, but published a few days after in the newspapers) it is stated that when Mgr. Satolli's document had been perused by the archbishops, they suggested some modifications, which the papal delegate may loathe to accept. Since at the request of all the members of the conference, he afterwards consented to alter the last sentence of his pamphlet, which now winds up by saying that it 'was read and considered in the meeting of the archbishops, the difficulty answered and the requisite alterations made.' Not a word to indicate that the metropolitans approved or accepted the document read to them. In the printed pamphlet no trace is found of those questions concerning Catholic and public schools that were the subject of the wide and violent discussions started by the Faribault and similar plans. That controversy is *not* settled.

"To maintain or insinuate that Leo XIII has in this matter spoken as 'the mouthpiece of the Church' is to ignore entirely the principle of Catholic theology. When the Church speaks through its head, the pope, his utterance is infallible, and no council of bishops, archbishops, patriarchs and cardinals would dare to reject his declaration or even most respectfully to offer a few amendments. If the Holy Father chooses at some future time to take this school question into his own hands and settle it finally by his supreme authority for the whole country, as he has settled it provisionally for two local cases, the bishops of America will obey, whatever his decision may be. But till then they as well as their flocks are bound by the decrees of the council of Baltimore; for as Mgr. Satolli observed in the New York conference, (see official report page 4) they are most wise decrees and, as far as they give a general rule of conduct, must be faithfully complied with, although their application in special circumstances must be left to the discretion of the several bishops. So much, then, is finally settled by the pope's representative, although not by an infallible authority. Yet, strange to say, some people are bound to see in Mgr. Satolli's address a complete overthrow of the Baltimore legislation, a reformed program of our Catholic school system, in fact the abolition of parochial schools. It is the old story: their eyes see what their hearts desire.

"Everybody will agree with the observation 'that the authority with which he (Mgr. Satolli) is invested, is unusual'. Certainly; and it does seem very improbable that the Holy See would entrust the most extraordinary and unusual power of settling finally and without appeal all ecclesiastical controversies and disputes arising in our land to a prelate, no matter how great his piety and learning, who is a perfect stranger in the country and to whom clergy and laymen must explain their business in Latin or Italian if they wish to be understood. Prominent Catholic churchmen have more than once openly declared that it requires a long time and close attention before a foreigner begins to understand the peculiar condition and character of American ecclesiastical affairs.

"The interview states that 'the papal representative has the further mission to inform himself accurately about American ecclesiastical matters in general and to report thereon *regularly* to Rome. *As time goes on,* he will receive other specific powers.' Does this mean a permanent Roman delegation with us? If so, we expect again that this question is not yet settled. Although the archbishops were told plainly of the pope's desire to have such a delegation established here, they did not feel warranted to act in so important a matter in view of the serious difficulty connected with the subject, as the report states. They were wise, indeed. To guard the future residing delegate from undue party-influence would not be the least nor the last among those difficulties. For party spirit apparently attempts to enter into American ecclesiastical life as it does into our politics. This leads to another subject.

"In your introductory remarks to Archbishop Ireland's interview, reference is made to Cahenslyism, and Mgr. Ireland is called its 'successful opponent'. Now, first of all, allow me to state that there is no connection whatever between the Cahensly movement and our school question. You were probably misled by the curious fact that the few Catholic weeklies that are in favor of state schools versus parochial schools, are also the loudest in denouncing Cahenslyism.

"So much paper and ink has been wasted on this subject in our newspapers and weeklies and stately reviews, that a few words may not be amiss. I am fully informed of the whole Cahensly movement and have all the documents referring to it in my hands. First, then, Cahenslyism as opposed by Archbishop Ireland and his followers is a bugbear. It does not exist in reality, never did. The phantom was called forth from its dark hiding place for a set purpose, and by constant misrepresentation it is still being kept before the American public and our English speaking Catholics for the same purpose, contrary to truth, charity, and the best interests of the Catholic Church in America. The continued cry of a 'Luzern Conspiracy', or of 'foreign political interference' in our ecclesiastical affairs, or of a 'double or multiple jurisdiction' according to the various nationalities, or of the overponderance of 'foreigners' as against 'Americans' in our hierarchy, is the utterance either of a man suffering from hallucination or of an evil mind. Those who in good earnest and sincerity of heart continue to battle against so-called Cahenslyism are an American variety of the good old chevalier, Don Quixote. Second: the memorial presented to the Holy See (not to Triple Alliance) by the St. Raphael's Societies of Italy, France, Germany and other countries through Mr. Cahensly, their delegate, was nothing more than an attempt to provide with the help and approval of the highest *ecclesiastical* (not political) power more ample and efficient measures for the spiritual and religious care of Catholic emigrants coming from those countries to our shores. True, some statements in the now famous memorial to the effect that an astonishing number of immigrants had lost the Catholic faith because they had not been sufficiently provided with priests able to speak their native languages, seemed greatly exaggerated to persons not fully acquainted with the real state of things or unwilling to admit the truth. Some would even see therein a serious charge against the American bishops as if they had negected their duty toward Catholic immigrants. It is evidently this charge unjustly drawn from the statements contained in the Cahensly memorial, that the archbishops in New York intended to refute in a letter sent to His Holiness. Again, the Raphael societies made the serious mistake of starting such an important movement without first consulting the American hierarchy on the subject. It was a blunder, not a crime; our German American Raphael society protested immediately against it. But as far as the real and main object of the Cahensly movement is concerned, it was acknowledged as most praiseworthy by the Holy See; its originators and patrons are too well known in Europe as intelligent, honest, and loyal Catholic gentlemen to allow any American to charge them with the intention of unduly interfering in our church affairs. It is gratifying, indeed, to see that our best Catholic papers written in English take a more sensible and Christian view of the subject than the noisy opponents of so-called 'Cahenslyism' have done. The ghost of Cahenslyism is dead. Let it rest in peace."

Episcopal statements on such controversial subjects merited brisk circulation. The *Milwaukee Sentinel* commented on them and Father Gmeiner of the St. Paul Archdiocese provided the *Sentinel* with a counterblast. The *Gazette,* January 11, 1893, copied it with the introductory note: "It is to be regretted that the Reverend Father's language is not couched more courteously." Gmeiner wondered whether Messmer really knew what he was talking about. The Confederates had planned to split the country only into two parts whereas the Cahenslyites wanted to split it into several dependencies. Moreover it was "nonsense to say that the Bennett law invaded the rights of parents or of conscience. The real objection to it in certain quarters was that by the insisting on the right of every child in the state to learn sufficiently the language of this country, the attachment to the 'mother country' on the other side of the ocean and the clannishness of the foreign colonists on American soil would gradually be dissolved. It is yet to be learned whether Wisconsin is still sufficiently American to restore again that law which foreign-minded dictators have flung to the winds with the aid of office-seeking American politicians."

Midsummer of 1893 brought a letter from the Vatican to Cardinal Gibbons assuring the hierarchy that the Baltimore legislation respecting parochial schools remained in force. The letter confirmed a similar one which Archbishop Corrigan received the foregoing year. This elated Messmer and just before school opened he issued a strong letter on parochial schools incorporating parts of the papal letter.[15] Right at the beginning he made a frontal attack on those who passed as liberals in the American Church.

---

[15]*Milwaukee Sentinel,* Aug. 31, 1893.

"Liberalizing opinions," said he, "always injurious to the true Catholic interests; sentimental phrases of closer communication with our separated brethren, appeals to a false and unreal American patriotism, lying charges of foreign and disloyal nationalism, highflown and indiscriminate praise of the public school system together with a scornful and unfair criticism of our parochial schools, a hypocritical sympathy with the poor 'double-tax' ridden Catholics, even the silly spectre of a conflict with the political powers—all this was brought into play to make the Catholics of this country understand that parochial schools, Catholic schools, were no longer opportune."[16]

Messmer referred to a "perverse interpretation of some propositions of the papal delegate" which led some people to believe that the pope had changed the laws of Baltimore so that Catholic parents were free to patronize the public schools. Messmer advised his clients to be guided by the papal letter; not by press dispatches, nor by clerical lecturers with self-assumed authority, nor by reports of interviews with priests notorious for their opposition to the bishop, nor by Catholic papers which played into the hands of the liberals.

Harking back a full century the bishop linked the common school without religion to the infidel principles of the French Revolution which separated the child from the family and alienated the school from both the family and the Church. This comment offers a significant insight into Messmer's mental make-up. Most German Catholics of the middle third of the century grew up in an atmosphere of reaction to the Revolution with its many implications. This made them extremely conservative, and Catholics of other lineages could not understand their attitude.

Messmer declared that public schools without religion are of their very nature dangerous to the Catholic faith. Second, where there is a Catholic school, parents must patronize it. Third, they may use public schools in cases of necessity provided they

---

[16]James H. Moynihan, *The Life of Archbishop John Ireland* (New York, 1953), p. 103, erroneously ascribes this to Katzer. The *Northwestern Chronicle* made the mistake and Moynihan copied it.

use all means to counteract danger to the faith. Fourth, it belongs to the bishop to decide when it is morally impossible to maintain a Catholic school and whether the proper safeguards have been taken.

Some Catholic papers had alleged that the Church never condemned the public schools. Messmer stoutly maintained she "must by her very mission condemn what is dangerous to the Catholic faith". Of course, he added, this condemnation pertained only to the public school as a means of educating Catholics. To have neutral state schools for the citizens of many different religions was another matter. "This condemnation", he continued, "of the system of 'public common schools' is a purely religious question. The Church does not concern herself with the different methods or systems of teaching followed in those schools; nor even directly with the various branches taught, or the teachers employed. The religious or irreligious character, the Christian or un-Christian atmosphere, the Catholic or non-Catholic spirit of the institution is the only foundation upon which the Church bases her judgment as to whether her children shall frequent the school or not; whether that school is to be condemned or not."

The letter was clearly belligerent, and the secular press recognized it as such. The *Milwaukee Sentinel* carried it in full and devoted an editorial to it. Still smarting from the repeal of the Bennett law, the editor recalled that the Church had harped on the rights of parents to educate their children as they saw fit. Churchmen had fulminated against the stipulations which "the people of the state, acting through their constituted authorities" laid down respecting education "to fit the child for the duties of citizenship". Now Messmer claimed the parents had no such right to determine the matter. Parental rights do not exist. The bishops and clergy decide. Yet the bishop discredits the liberal clergy from judging.

Messmer at once wrote to the *Sentinel* and referred to the Bennett law by name. He also mentioned the attack made on himself by the *Daily Northwestern* of Oshkosh which spoke of tyranny and "out-Bennetting" the Bennett law. The *Sentinel* carried his letter in full and devoted an editorial to it.[17] The editor conceded the great value of first impressions in educating children and of having them "in a school where the tenets and rites of the Catholic Church are made the foremost object of instruction and reverence". He continued to quote Messmer as saying that God had a right to interfere with the rights of parents in the choice of schools and he quipped that Messmer was "on such terms with the Supreme Being that his instructions are to be received as the commands of God." If the bishop had the power there would be no schools except those controlled by his church.

Another letter from the bishop and another editorial followed. Avowing that the clergy are as human and as power thirsty as politicians the *Sentinel* assured the reading public that "it is not reasonable to accept all their decisions as sanctified by divine authority".[18] The same issue carried the bishop's letter which deprecated the omnipotence of the state. He again classed the Bennett law as a socio-political problem and gibed that if a citizen pays the school tax he should be provided with the kind of school that he can use "without infringing on the right of his Creator." He referred again to the French Revolution, this time characterizing socialism and communism as its daughters.

Other papers also had their say. The *Janesville Gazette* charged: "Bishop Messmer takes upon himself a power which he denies to the state under its right of self preservation."[19] The *Manitowoc Pilot* said Messmer's letter hardly added to his reputation.[20] The editor regretted that he had emphasized the need of isolating Catholics and had allied himself with the enemies of the public schools. He referred passingly to Messmer's reputation as a liberal in contrast to Katzer who opposed all liberalizing influences and he couldn't help but wonder just why saloons and dance halls were not condemned as emphatically as the public school.

---

[17]*Milwaukee Sentinel*, Sept. 3, 1893.
[18]*Ibid.*, Sept. 7, 1893.
[19]Quoted in Fond du Lac *Commonwealth*, Sept. 15, 1893.
[20]*Milwaukee Sentinel*, Sept. 10, 1893.

According to the *Two Rivers Chronicle* Messmer feared public schools only when they directly competed with parochial schools. "If Catholic children are to be driven from public schools when parochial schools are equally as convenient, why not drive Catholic teachers therefrom also? It is not to the credit of any church to allow its communicants to teach to other children what it refuses to let them teach to its own."[21] Somewhat similarly the *Appleton Post* wrote: "If a protest is ever registered against the employment of Catholic teachers in our public schools the cause will be traced directly to the war made upon them by just such fanatical zealots as Bishop Messmer whose religion appears to be an amalgam of greed and gospel."[22]

Even the *Catholic Citizen*,[23] without naming names, carried an editorial hardly favorable to the bishop. The editor saw in the world "compromisers and zealots". Some made a "fad" out of the parish school and wanted heresy trials and political quarrels. The *Northwestern Chronicle*,[24] erroneously reporting the pastoral as a composition of Katzer, characterized it as "the stalking horse for a bitter attack on the so-called American wing of the Catholic Church. . . . When there is no sacrifice of truth or principle, how can liberal opinions injuriously affect Catholic interests? Is the Church to move only in the low lands of narrowness, intolerance, and stagnation? . . . Is the prosperity of the Church based upon isolation and hate?"

Those who were not following this battle of words probably were following Archbishop Satolli across the nation to Chicago where he delivered an address at the Catholic Congress. After that Archbishop Katzer escorted him to Milwaukee. Then the delegate continued northward to Green Bay where Bishop Messmer saluted him in Latin and observed all the rubrical formalities. On the feast of the Nativity of the Blessed Virgin the delegate sang a pontifical Mass at St. Joseph's Church in De Pere before

---

[21] Quoted in *Oshkosh Weekly Northwestern*, Sept. 23, 1893.
[22] *Idem.*
[23] Sept. 9, 1893.
[24] Sept. 15, 1893.

a vast audience which included almost every priest of the diocese. The conservative Wisconsinite and the Roman, whose views were thought to be somewhat liberal, made northeastern Wisconsin conscious of the splendor of the Church, its prodigious growth, and its close union with the see of Peter.

A year later the *American Ecclesiastical Review* carried Messmer's article, "A Catholic Temperance League", inviting all enemies of the abuse of liquor to join a society which would have for its goal temperance rather than total abstinence. Having been subject for some time to Bishop Keane, a conspicuous crusader for abstinence, Messmer enjoyed pointing out that such a program would never appeal to Catholics who spoke languages other than English. "That exaggerated and un-Catholic temperance doctrine", he wrote, "which would make teetotalism an article of faith and a moral obligation for everybody, and force its pledge on all, casting indirectly a slur on every temperate drinker, has done more to render the word 'temperance' odious among thousands of temperate and intemperate Catholics immigrated here from continental Europe, than persons unacquainted with their ideas and feelings can imagine. It has made the so-called 'temperance people' a laughing stock to them and rendered the very best among continental Catholics suspicious of every temperance movement."

Messmer thought the league could oppose the adulteration of drinks and the custom of gambling for liquor. It could also promote legislation to control the liquor industry. However, the *Bulletin* of the Catholic Total Abstinence Union scrapped the proposal summarily: "The question of forming a temperance league which all Catholic friends of temperance could join, has been broached in some quarters. The Catholic Total Abstinence Union cannot modify its principles to become a member of such a league. The vice of intemperance can be overcome only by total abstinence; it is the efficacious remedy."[25]

Being an admirer of the St. Raphael Society, Messmer deemed it advisable to develop rural Catholic colonies. Hatred of Cahensly

---

[25] Joan Bland, *Hibernian Crusade The Story of the Catholic Total Abstinence Union of America* (Washington, 1951), pp. 191-192.

caused the program to be shelved, but in 1895 Messmer urged the state branch of the Central Verein to interest itself in "a thorough Catholic rural life". Good land was disappearing from the market but he thought some could be found if an agent in every county were on the alert for possibilities. Little eventuated but in 1903 Messmer was still sufficiently interested to establish an Immigrant and Land Bureau to issue descriptive pamphlets to lure German immigrants to Wisconsin.[26]

Messmer also served as chairman of the executive committee of the Catholic Colonization Society[27] and in that capacity he issued an explanatory pamphlet, dated February 26, 1912. He declared that the archbishops at their annual meeting endorsed the organization. Among its objectives was the formation of racial colonization societies. Said Messmer: "However much we may desire the quick and full amalgamation and merging of such races in the American nation, it cannot possibly be denied that for a time racial settlements and colonies are necessary, if these newcomers to our shores are to keep the Catholic faith themselves and help to build up a glorious future of the Church in America.... The Catholic Colonization Society will arrange with the land company for the building of an appropriate church and school and parsonage to be erected within a certain time or as soon as a given number of Catholic families shall have settled there. The land company must, moreover, guarantee the salary of a priest for a certain time to be agreed upon."

As archbishop of Milwaukee he addressed the Wisconsin Country Life Conference on: "Some Moral Aspects of Country Life." Very philosophically and no less charmingly he argued that country life was more conducive to morality than city life. According to him a farmer has two duties: religion and work. The former is a tribute of his whole being to God whereas work indirectly helps and safeguards his morality. The archbishop

---

[26]Barry, *op. cit.*, p. 255.

[27]This society, incorporated in Illinois, July, 1911, succeeded a former organization of the same name.

argued that the family, the foundation of the state, is inviolable and has the duty of educating children. Yet the world suffers from two fatal errors: the state is the great and primary educator and education may be attained without religion. Farmers in his eyes have an ideal opportunity to grow strong from simple food and plenty of exercise. On a higher plane they have the advantage of studying nature's secrets without herbariums and laboratories. Nature, in turn, imposes a regular pattern of daily life on them. If ignored, the fields and herds withhold their treasures. Lastly, farmers are frugal and thrifty, perhaps too thrifty, and they are conservative in contrast to city people who readily experiment with social revolution.

It was while Messmer presided over Green Bay that Wisconsin enacted a new law concerning marriage licenses. Realizing the importance of this legislation, Messmer issued a letter on May 5, 1899, summarizing its requirements. As a former professor of Canon Law it was natural for him to add a discussion of the Church's laws on impediments, declaration of nullity, fictitious consent, the publication of the banns, and so forth. At some other time before leaving Green Bay he produced a compact pamphlet of twenty-six pages entitled *Pastoral Instruction on Christian Marriage* which also appeared in French and in German.[28]

Although the bishop avoided politics, when Leon Colgosz assassinated President McKinley he stated in St. John's Church, Appleton, that it was a serious mistake to allow anarchists to hold meetings.[29] Their conventicles culminate in tragedy and people who tolerate such assemblies share the guilt. Then, also, when the ex-priest McGrady tried to confuse people about the nature of

---

[28] In 1924 he issued a pastoral on marriage which was entirely different from the earlier one.

In 1898 he issued *Notae ad Statuta Diocesana* touching on marriage laws, catechetical instruction, business administration, salaries, singing in the vernacular at high Masses, and other irregularities.

[29] *Catholic Citizen*, Sept. 21, 1901.

socialism the bishop did not simply ignore him but wrote a letter forbidding his people to attend the lecture.[30]

Likewise, when Assemblyman Sweeting of Manitowoc County introduced a bill to remove the statue of Marquette from Statuary Hall in Washington, Messmer delivered a two-hour address on the subject in Marinette on February 14, 1897. In clear terms he traced the bill to bigotry saying: "The cry against that statue is the cry against the Catholic Church and its adherents. The party which attempts to cast the marble Jesuit out from the capitol is but driving out the American Catholics from the public and political life of the nation."

If Messmer became indignant at the thought of banishing the statue of Marquette from Washington, he was just as incensed when the superintendent of schools in Outagamie County notified several sisters teaching in public schools that they would lose their teacher's certificates. Messmer gave this opinion to the press: "I do not think that our state laws forbid district boards to allow Catholic teachers to give religious instruction either before or after the regular school hours to those children whose parents desire it so long as no tax-payer of that district objects to such an arrangement. If this were against the law, how could the use of the public schools be allowed for Sunday services and Sunday schools as is done not unfrequently." Messmer argued: "All the work which the state demands of its schools is done; what right has the state to forbid the other work as long as the citizens and parents concerned desire it? Suppose it were an extra class in drawing or manual work. Would the state interfere with the district? What right has it to interfere because the citizens without exception or objection want this class to be religion? Must religion then be banished even where all citizens interested in the school demand it?"

The same year that Messmer came to Green Bay the first Catholic Summer School met in New London, Connecticut. Not-

---

[30] *Literary Digest*, April 12, 1902, p. 508. In 1902 a Socialist monthly, *The Vanguard*, began appearing in Green Bay. McGrady was among its contributors.

withstanding the academic name, it consisted merely of lectures on subjects that interest Catholics. Combining instruction with recreation and travel the project immediately gained popularity in the east. One day a few literati met at Dr. Egan's cottage near Notre Dame University and decided to arrange a similar event in the west. Madison was selected as the site for the annual meetings which began in 1895. Although very successful, the initial series of lectures set off such repercussions that securing speakers for the ensuing years became difficult.

It so happened that Father Zahm of Notre Dame, the chairman of the committee on study and lectures, invited O'Gorman and Pace of the Catholic University to deliver some lectures. Messmer, the president of the organization, had not been consulted. Upon hearing of this arrangement he wrote to O'Gorman on January 20, 1896:

"We laid it down as a rule last year not to engage, or invite any professor from the University for our platform. Again, having been exposed to a great deal of incrimination last year on account of Dr. Zahm's expression on the evolution of man, we have to be much more careful this year to have no theories or opinions put forth from our boards which would not find acceptance with all. For this reason myself and others objected at once to arrangement made by Dr. Zahm. But to relieve him of his delicate position we compromised by instructing him to inform you of the sentiments of the board and to ask you—in case you still desire to lecture to us—to choose a subject where there will be no danger of advancing theories or opinions which would or might involve the school into difficulties or controversies."[31]

The same day Messmer asked Pace to cancel his engagement explaining that: "Whatever each one's private opinion may be, the fact cannot be denied that the Catholic University and its professors and rector are not looked upon with favor by many of our Catholics."[32]

---

[31] Ahern, *op. cit.*, pp. 157-158.
[32] *Ibid.*, p. 158.

Zahm, nursing a bruised ego, lost no time in prodding Pace on to ignore Messmer. He had arrogated to himself undue authority and jeopardized the interests of the University. Messmer was no doubt chagrined when he learned that O'Gorman had become bishop of Sioux Falls,[33] but he could not have been surprised that Keane turned against him. By way of compensation he found solace in the fact that just then the apostolic delegate was slowly withdrawing from the liberals and moving toward the conservatives. More than that, Keane was removed in brusque fashion from the rectorship. Four years later—as archbishop of Dubuque —he came uncomfortably close to Green Bay.

In the interim Messmer visited Rome. O'Connell of the American College shadowed him and reported back to the States that he feared the worst because the bishop of Green Bay talked much against Heckerism to the pope, the cardinals, and the Jesuits. In line with the convictions which he voiced in Rome, Messmer signed the joint letter of the bishops of the Milwaukee province charging that unorthodox Americanism percolated through the United States, but since the opponents of this minority view vented their wrath primarily upon Katzer his suffragans escaped obloquy.

If the old century closed with something so old as a controversy about orthodoxy, the new one brought with it something new which owed much to Messmer and James McFaul, an alumnus of Seton Hall, who became bishop of Trenton. It was the Federation of Catholic Societies. In structure it resembled the Central Verein and its lectures paralleled those of the defunct Catholic Summer School. Rather belligerently McFaul charged: "American citizens, because they are Catholics, are discriminated against, and we are determined to unite for the purpose of defending ourselves. . . . My experience leads me to the conclusion that a policy of silence has been very detrimental to our interests."[34]

---

[33] *Ibid.*, p. 158. According to Ireland strenuous efforts were made to bar O'Gorman from the episcopate.

[34] James A. McFaul, "Catholics and American Citizenship", *North American Review*, Sept., 1900, pp. 320-332; John Tracy Ellis, *The Life of*

Churchmen such as Ireland carped that the Federation would grow into a political party like the Center in Germany. McFaul and Messmer could deftly rebut by quoting Pope Leo's recent encyclical on Christian democracy, dated January 18, 1901. After reprobating bitter disputes and subtle, useless discussions the pope added: "The action of Catholics, of whatever sort, will proceed with a larger effectiveness, if all their associations, while the rights of each one remain secure, have one and the same directing and moving force at their head."

However, fear of socialism, more so than this recommendation, prompted the Federation. Here again Leo XIII blazed the trail in the very first year of his pontificate by issuing *Quod Apostolici Muneris* on Marxism. Furthermore, the recent attacks on the Church by the A. P. A. as well as the religious difficulties concerning the Indian schools and the war with Spain pointed up the need for Catholic enlightenment followed by Catholic action.

At the Federation's first convention in 1901 the rector of St. Peter's Cathedral in Cincinnati spoke on socialism. Simultaneously the Central Verein launched a drive for members with a view to forming distinctively Catholic unions of workingmen.[35] Messmer declared the industrial and social question to be one of the most

---

James Cardinal Gibbons Archbishop of Baltimore 1834-1921 (Milwaukee, 1952), vol. II, pp. 375-378; Mary Harrita Fox, *Peter E. Dietz Labor Priest* (Notre Dame, 1953), pp. 18-19, 34-35; James H. Moynihan, *The Life of Archbishop John Ireland* (New York, 1953), pp. 285-286; *Catholic Citizen*, June 18, 1904, characterized the Federation as an offshoot of the Central Verein and referred to the question of a Catholic party.

[35] According to *The Telegraph* (Cincinnati), Dec. 5, 1901, Bishop Spalding said of the Christian Democracy movement: "Concerning the efforts to induce Catholics to withdraw from labor unions which are dominated by anarchistic or socialistic ideas and aims, I will say that such a movement must result in good, especially if it is promoted by the German and Polish Catholic societies. They are strong, firmly united and deeply influenced by religious motives. A radical distinction must be drawn between socialism and anarchism, but in this country socialism is advocated chiefly by those who are hostile to religion and to some of the fundamental principles of civilized life, and hence it is our duty both as Christians and good citizens to do what we can to counteract the baleful influence of their propaganda."

important confronting Catholic laymen. Asserting that labor unions all rested on the principles of socialism, he contended that soon Catholics would not be able to join them. America would have to follow the example of Germany, France, Belgium, and Spain in forming unions based on principles of Christian society and on the tenets of Leo's *Rerum Novarum*.[36]

A few months after airing his views in Ohio he repeated his plea for the Federation in Oshkosh at a convention of mutual aid and youth societies of Wisconsin and upper Michigan. He went to Cleveland to address a meeting of the Central Verein and he highlighted a convention of the Catholic Knights of Wisconsin in Sheboygan. Messmer told the Knights: "No Catholic can ever accept the principles of socialism, and there is no dispute over it any more and no doubt. . . . In most of the labor unions, and those being started today, there is the socialistic principle. . . . The fact is simply this, that if the labor unions will adopt those principles of socialism, no Catholic can belong to them." He urged Catholics to exert their influence on those unions which could be kept free from socialism so that Catholics could join them with a safe conscience as in Germany, where Catholics and other Christians collaborate to combat socialist infiltration. "We, as Catholics," said he, "must do something, and we must make a beginning in taking hold of this particular question, the labor question."[37]

The same year, 1902, saw Messmer in Chicago preaching at the pontifical Mass for the Federation's second convention. The delegates passed resolutions on the Philippine question and on Catholic high schools. They sympathized with the Catholic Indian schools which had lost the favor of Washington. Likewise with

---

[36]*The Telegraph*, December 19, 1901. In 1904 the delegates endorsed trade unions to better the material condition of workingmen but exhorted Catholics to form special associations to provide for religious and moral needs and instruct the members on the social question.

[37]*Proceedings of the Ninth Biennial State Council, Catholic Knights of Wisconsin* (Oshkosh, 1902), pp. 19-32. The Knights did not share Messmer's enthusiasm for the Federation because they feared political entanglements.

the religious orders which just then were suffering persecution in France. Archbishop Ireland, who was lionized alike in Paris and Washington, criticized the stand taken by the Catholic press and by some societies. Far from intimidating Messmer, this goaded him to declare that the Federation would brook no dictation from anyone regarding its right to discuss the Philippine question. "This may be considered a rebuke to Archbishop Ireland, and it may be not." McFaul supported Messmer with a spirited address on the Philippine question and the opinion gained credence that had the Federation existed at the time of the war with Spain, the situation might not have become as grave as it did.

Messmer attained national fame through the Federation so when Archbishop Katzer died in 1903 the Holy See advanced him to the metropolitan see. Messmer and his predecessor had much in common. Katzer was an Austrian by birth; Messmer had studied in Austria. Both had been professors in America; both were conservative; both advanced from Green Bay to Milwaukee. Messmer, however, was more scholarly, more diplomatic, and more at ease in the company of distinguished people.

One thing was to distinguish Messmer's accession from that of Katzer. The latter, as well as Heiss and Henni, had received the pallium with impressive ceremonies and in Katzer's case with too much adverse publicity. Messmer dispensed with all pomp by delegating Msgr. George Jacquemin of the Anima College to receive it vicariously in Rome. It arrived in Milwaukee by mail and Messmer donned it without further ado.[38]

About the same time that Messmer became a metropolitan O'Connell became rector of the Catholic University. Twenty years ago the two had worked side by side at the council of Baltimore. The former had watched this protege of Gibbons rise to head the American College in Rome; he also saw him removed in uncomplimentary fashion. Owing to their common background the new archbishop felt free to speak his mind candidly to him on January 26, 1904. "I was angry with you," he wrote, "very angry, for the

---

[38]*Catholic Citizen*, Dec. 31, 1904.

prominent and active part you took in the so-called liberal movement of American prelates. Common report, never contradicted, had it that you were the most active and influential agent of that party in Rome. True, I never doubted your good intention, but on the other hand I had my firmly set convictions regarding the consequences of that movement upon the Church in America. As I thought and felt, so felt thousands of our German Catholics, as you know. Your appointment as rector of the University came as a shock to them, when they had just somewhat recovered from the resentment against the University caused by the treatment of Dr. Schroeder (God rest his soul). But I am glad to say that the assurances publicly made immediately after your appointment by men connected with the University that henceforth the management of that institution would show more consideration towards the views and feelings of the German Catholics, and especially that the officials and professors of the University would keep off from any party movements in the American Church, has put a quietus upon their fears."[39]

Messmer hastened to approve the suggestion that a German-American priest serve as vice-rector, and he submitted several names for the position. None was appointed, and many German groups continued unfriendly to the University. Messmer further recommended that the professors avoid civil and ecclesiastical politics but two years later both he and Ireland curtly informed the University that they would not send any more priest-students. The proper training simply was not available.[40] Messmer then went on to cite the decree of the president of the University of Wisconsin, Charles Van Hise, that no professor could do outside work such as tutoring or practise law and retain his position on the faculty.

Writing to Gibbons, Messmer said he heard that O'Connell interfered too much. "He may have too small or narrow an idea of a university professor and its faculty. They ought to be given

---

[39] Colman Barry, *The Catholic University of America 1903-1909 The Rectorship of Denis J. O'Connell* (Washington, 1950), p. 200.

[40] *Ibid.*, p. 175.

the greatest liberty, and the several faculties ought to enjoy as much 'home rule' as possible."[41]

A few months earlier he had deprecated all petty, vexatious tyranny. According to him: "While each professor controls his own class, the collective work is controlled by the faculties, not by the rector nor by anyone on the staff. The senate and faculties make the laws and rules for the university and the several departments; the rector will direct their execution. I often think the rector's position is much like that of the president of the United States. Nor is he a mere executive. He makes the rules and issues orders; but under the laws. He may and ought often to take the initiative in proposing new legislation, general or specific; but he leaves it to congress to decide."[42]

Messmer co-operated with the University all the while he criticized it. He served on the board of trustees, spoke on its behalf, and attended conventions of the Catholic Educational Association which was a scion of the University. Conspicuous on the Association's agenda for 1907 was the care of Catholic students at secular colleges.[43] Father John Farrell had counseled students at Harvard for eight years and he inspired others to extend the apostolate to other colleges. While many straddled the issue or flatly condemned Catholic halls as compromises with secular education Bishop McQuaid completed plans for one at Cornell,[44] and in 1906 Archbishop Messmer deputed Father Hengell to care for the students at the University of Wisconsin. These men realized the importance of a state university and maintained that caring for the souls of students would not undermine the Catholic University or any Catholic college any more than the Confraternity of Christian Doctrine sabotages parochial schools by instructing public school pupils. Although some parishes made niggardly con-

---

[41] *Ibid.*, p. 139, n. 90.

[42] *Ibid.*, pp. 138-139.

[43] *Ibid.*, pp. 227-228.

[44] Rev. Peter Dietz of Oberlin carried on a controversy on this subject in *The Catholic Universe* in 1907. It was reprinted in booklet form, *The Catholic Hall.*

tributions, Messmer avowed in a public letter dated November 15, 1921, that the obligation of supporting St. Paul's Chapel at Madison "lies nearer to us than the duty of helping the Catholic University at Washington."

Besides shepherding the Catholic students at Wisconsin, Messmer was a friend of Marquette. When the Jesuits raised its status from that of a college to a university he wrote: "Milwaukee should welcome such a branching out as is suggested for Marquette College. A university leaves an impress upon the entire community. Madison University is too far away from Milwaukee for this city to reap the full benefits to be derived from the atmosphere of that institution. But in Madison everyone is benefited by the presence of the university in that city. What a state university does for Madison, a university located here would do for Milwaukee. No need of the city is greater than the need for a university or better facilities for higher education."[45]

As a genuine university man he kept an interest in scholarship throughout life. At Seton Hall he wrote and as bishop he kept his pen busy. He contributed a few brief items to *The Catholic Encyclopedia,* he wrote for the *Catholic Historical Review,* he published Durward's sketch of Father Kundig in the *Salesianum,* and he edited the works of Bishop England which fill seven large volumes. In 1903 he edited Devivier's *Christian Apologetics: A Defence of the Catholic Faith* but Miss Ella McMahon was responsible for the translating. He edited *Spirago's Method of Christian Doctrine for Priests, Teachers and Parents,* but again someone else did the translating. In 1910 he published *Outlines of Bible Knowledge,* based upon Andrew Bruell's *Bibelkunde,* and in 1927 a second revised edition appeared. It is of interest to note that the preface to the first edition praised the studies of Gigot and Breen. The latter had in 1907 caused a furor in the diocese of Rochester by attacking Father Hanna as doctrinally unfit for the episcopate. Messmer ultimately rescued Breen from

---

[45]Gilbert J. Garraghan, *The Jesuits of the Middle United States* (New York, 1938), vol. III, p. 454.

oblivion by giving him a professorship at St. Francis Seminary which he held down to his death in 1938. Conversely Breen relieved Messmer who temporarily taught Scripture at the seminary owing to some local difficulties at St. Francis.[46]

Being endowed with a penchant for history the archbishop took an active interest in the Wisconsin Historical Society and served on its board of curators. Those who use its library find an occasional reminder of his culture in the stamp "The Archbishop Messmer Binding Fund". In his private capacity he asked priests to send him old Catholic directories, souvenir books, and jubilee books. Even financial reports, he observed, could be of service to historians. He himself would pay the cost of transportation to build up the archives of the diocese. Unfortunately for historiographers either Messmer's papers perished or they are cached away by someone who enjoys seeing historians seek and knock in vain. That the archbishop acquired some significant items is beyond doubt but, in general, his forte was thinking, not organizing. "That's a capital idea", pronounced with a slight brogue, was one of his pet phrases. Needless to say, not every one of them materialized.

Many claim that Messmer gathered data on Cahenslyism. It seems, however, that these rumors resulted from jovial raconteuring with the refrain: "I could write something about that." Even in his prime Messmer was not original and as he advanced in age one of the charges leveled against him was his dilatory handling of all business. It is unlikely that he was simultaneously doing careful research in so secretive a way as to evade the notice of his intimate associates. However, a letter to Father Markert, written on February 14, 1926, proves that he was not just talking because in it he outlined some research to be done in Rome and Baltimore.[47]

Messmer's hobby of reading abstracts and delving into documents was widely known. Consequently Cardinal Gibbons ex-

---

[46] *Salesianum*, Oct., 1953, pp. 172-179.

[47] The Ms. is in possession of the writer.

pressed the opinion that he would be the logical man to solicit funds from the American bishops to help Ludwig von Pastor when the latter was in need after the defeat of Austria. His Eminence offered to start the fund with a contribution of $100. Instead of repartee, the archbishop chose procrastination. Finally, upon learning that Gibbons meanwhile asked another to take up the project, Messmer assured the cardinal: "I am very glad that Bishop Muldoon is going to take charge of it. It will come with far better grace from Bishop Muldoon than it would come from me, who stands before the public as a German, though I am a Swiss."[48]

Despite his interest in the past Messmer realized the necessity of influencing public opinion and of providing enlightened leadership in the new field of sociology. For that reason he pushed the American Federation of Catholic Societies while he was still bishop of Green Bay. Although the Federation had recommended the study of *Rerum Novarum* at its very first convention, it shied away from endorsing labor unions. The leaders thought the Church could help the working class without the aid of unions. However, owing in part to Father Dietz, a change occurred. This native New Yorker, who had made some of his studies abroad, pioneered in preaching social reform. After leaving the Central Verein he rose to prominence in the Federation. In 1910 he attended the A. F. of L. convention in St. Louis as its fraternal delegate. Impressed by what he saw and heard, he organized Catholic trade unionists under the title "Militia of Christ." Their slogan "Thy kingdom come" was to enkindle a spirit of enterprise rather than resignation. Messmer disliked the title because it sounded like some pious sodality and offered an opportunity for ridicule. Though altered to American Conference of Catholic Trade Unionists this cumbersome designation got little circulation. Down through the years dynamic Dietz remained a bosom friend of Messmer, and, when difficulties with Archbishop Moeller har-

---

[48]*Catholic Historical Review*, Oct., 1948, pp. 306-318. Messmer, Mundelein, and Muldoon were on the committee of the American hierarchy to send relief to the victims of the war.

assed him in Ohio, he found a welcome in Milwaukee. Here was a friendship that thrived on dissimilarity. Dietz, the young crusader, had no *Gemuetlichkeit;* Messmer, the seasoned administrator, had much. The latter's invitations to card games and causeries went unaccepted. Few could have plied the archbishop more, none exploited him less.[49]

The Federation languished from a lack of definite objectives but as late as 1913 it held a convention in Milwaukee under the aegis of Messmer. Both Gibbons and Ireland participated. The Federation continued down to the middle of World War I. Then the National Catholic War Council took over some of its work. After the war ended, this organization evolved into the N. C. W. C. and the Federation passed into history. Dietz, being *persona non grata,* was not appointed to any of its departments. Failing that, Messmer tried to get him a position in the Harding administration. He wrote to Senator Lenroot: "He has had remarkable success with a number of American labor organizations in holding them aloof from the more radical and socialistic influences. Among Catholics I know of no other man, priest or layman, who has such a thorough theoretical as well as practical knowledge of the labor question."[50] However, Dietz' career in sociology had ended. He ceded his school property in Ohio to the Catholic Students Mission Crusade, returned to Wisconsin, and organized St. Monica parish in Whitefish Bay where he remained until his death.

Besides sponsoring Father Dietz, Messmer promoted social thought in other ways. The Central Verein conducted courses at Spring Bank, and in his seminary Father Charles Bruehl taught sociology. This chair was held later by two prominent men whom Messmer sent away for further study: Bishop Francis J. Haas and Archbishop Aloysius J. Muench. The former went to Washington; the latter to Switzerland. Monsignor Matthew McEvoy, whom Messmer sent to the Catholic University, also propagated

---

[49] Fox, *op. cit.;* B. J. Blied, "Pioneer Social Reformer Rev. Peter E. Dietz", *Social Justice Review,* July-Aug., 1953, pp. 132-134.

[50] Fox, *op. cit.,* p. 201.

Christian ideals in the years that he presided over the Catholic Social Welfare Bureau in Milwaukee. Though this bureau dates from the final decade of Messmer's career and limits itself to a small sphere of activity, as far back as 1913 Messmer had appointed Dietz to organize the Milwaukee Conference of Catholic Charities and Social Service. Its purpose was to establish "a common centre for community and co-operation along parish lines; to collect and render centrally accessible all Catholic data bearing on charity and social work; to study social problems, to promote social reform and to take part in all social betterment activities." Despite the apt phraseology and the appointment of four basic committees on finance; relief; wages, housing, and health; and legislation; the program quickly fell into oblivion.

Newspaper work also enlisted the archbishop's support. He as well as the Federation recognized that the press could defend the Church as well as disseminate information. Back in 1888 Michael Kruszka began publishing the *Kuryer Polski* which, though not a Catholic paper, agitated for increased control of church affairs by the laity. Since the paper's subscribers were all Catholic, its policies affected church circles. The *Katolik* was founded to oppose it, but after three years it suspended publication. A subsequent publication survived six years only to go out of business with a huge deficit. In 1907, at the request of Messmer, the *Nowiny Polski* was founded to fight against the *Kuryer* and the Kruszkas. The archbishop himself contributed $1000 while the Polish pastors were assessed $500 each and their assistants $200.[51]

If the *Nowiny* survived the attacks made upon its editor, Father B. E. Goral, Messmer was far from finished with the *Kuryer*. The reason for this lay in the fact that the *Kuryer* kept up the agitation for a Polish bishop. As said above, just before

---

[51] *We the Milwaukee Poles: The History of Milwaukeeans of Polish Descent and a Record of their Contributions to the Greatness of Milwaukee* compiled by Thaddeus Borun (Milwaukee, 1946), p. 54. Edmund Olszyk, *The Polish Press in America* (Milwaukee, 1940), p. 43, concludes that 120 Polish publications were founded between 1870 and 1900. By 1905 only 49 remained. The *Kuryer's* advocacy of teaching Polish in the public schools was interpreted as an attack on parochial schools. *Ibid.*, p. 25.

the dawn of the twentieth century Vilatte machinated among disgruntled Poles in the larger cities who were amenable to schism and in 1903 Father Kruszka of the Milwaukee archdiocese took a petition to Rome asking for wider recognition of his fellow Poles.[52] This occurred precisely when both Katzer and Leo XIII died. A private letter of Messmer concerning the Federation, written shortly after he succeeded Katzer, has preserved his opinion at this stage of the controversy.

"I am extremely anxious to have the Polish people join—but their priests are in the way. One of the prominent Wisconsin Polish priests told me to my face 'It is all right for others to federate but we must keep our Polish folks away from the rest'. And how these men clamor for a bishop of their own nationality! To you in confidence: the more I think over this question the more I fear the consequences of appointing a Polish bishop anywhere in the United States. He will not be a bishop of his diocese but the bishop of the Poles in America; rest assured. Now when the time will come to show my position in the matter publicly it will turn the Polish against me and indirectly against the Federation. True, we can get along without them; but how much better it were to have them with us".[53]

On January 19, 1905, Messmer said the same to Gibbons: "There is a petition from the province of Milwaukee for a new diocese here. Now the paper brought the news today that the Polish are going to make new efforts to get one of their men elected bishop for the new diocese. The longer I think over it the more it seems to me a dangerous experiment at this stage to give the Polish people a bishop, for the very reason that he will be considered the bishop *for all the Poles* of the U.S. I know it. Wherever a bishop would have any difficulty with a Polish parish,

---

[52] The Latin text of this document appeared serially in *The Review* starting Oct. 8, 1903, p. 598. *Catholic Citizen*, May 14, 1904. *Columbia*, April 25, 1907, reported that Messmer wrote to Kruszka asking him to stop agitating publicly for a Polish bishop.

[53] Messmer to Arthur Preuss, Jan. 23, 1904. Ms. in the archives of the Central Verein.

their bishop would be appealed to. The Polish are not yet American enough and keep aloof too much from the rest of us."[54]

In 1907 Father Hodur climaxed his opposition to Rome by going to Utrecht for schismatic consecration and the next year the Vatican gave the Poles their first bishop by appointing Bishop Rhode an auxiliary in Chicago. Encouraged but not satisfied the *Kuryer* kept demanding more recognition. On October 10, 1911, twenty-five Polish priests met in Milwaukee and signed a document which, while repudiating the program of the *Kuryer,* asked for a Polish bishop in the archdiocese as a means of pacifying discontent. This happened less than six months after Messmer announced that he had assumed the debts of St. Josaphat's. Hence he was in no mood for compromise when he and his suffragans composed the letter condemning the *Kuryer* as "greatly injurious to Catholic faith and discipline and falling under the rules and prohibitions of the Roman Index." Under date of February 11, 1912, the bishops declared:

"The agitation for Polish bishops in the United States has assumed such a character, especially in our province, that it becomes positively subversive and destructive of Catholic faith, loyalty, discipline, and order. No sensible person will blame the Polish Catholics of America for being desirous of having bishops who can preach to them the word of God in their own mother tongue. Rome, with its wisdom gathered from the experience of over a thousand years and guided by the Spirit from on high, will know the time and the way to solve this important problem confronting the Church in America. Whenever and wherever the Holy See shall see fit to appoint Polish bishops in the United States, whether to residential sees or to the office of auxiliaries, the other bishops of the American Catholic hierarchy will receive them with sentiments of a true and loyal Catholic love and reverence. In the meantime, Polish Catholics may rest assured that the bishops of our hierarchy will be just as solicitous and zealous for the spiritual and ecclesiastical interests of the Polish faithful as they must

---

[54]Barry, *Church and German Americans,* p. 275.

be for all the other children of the Church, whatever their nationality or race. But Polish Catholics must also be persuaded that love of one's nation or race or tongue can not be allowed to degenerate into blind passion and narrow-minded sentiment, and that blind nationalism has been the cause of all the great and disastrous schisms in the history of the Church. . . .Where nationalism and nationalistic passions strive to become the leading and ruling principles in the affairs of the Church, general or local, they breathe and beget the spirit of disobedience and rebellion and very soon of heresy itself. When men of this spirit systematically attack the public acts of ecclesiastical superiors in the exercise of their lawful authority, they undermine that ecclesiastical authority itself and shatter the very foundation of rule and order in the Church. When in that same spirit they claim for the lay people the power of government in ecclesiastical affairs, and the right of management of the church properties, independent of the lawfully appointed bishops, they attack the very constitution and fundamental law upon which the visible organization of the Church is built. . . .

"The fight against what they maliciously call the 'German' bishops of this province of Milwaukee, is but a sham battle to cover the real fight for ecclesiastical independence from non-Polish bishops; the proposed appeal to the Holy Father himself as against the American bishops is but a device to deceive the unwary Polish faithful; even the words of the pope, reported by a clergyman as having been spoken to him some eight years ago, are being most shamefully misused for the purpose of poisoning the minds of Polish Catholics against the pope as being untrue to his word, and against American bishops as stopping the pope from keeping his promise."

As soon as the joint letter of the bishops appeared the *Kuryer* boasted of increased circulation, but before long it filed a suit for $100,000 against the bishops for boycotting the paper. On May 22, 1912, a group of Polish priests again met at Stevens Point and repeated the request for a Polish bishop. Meanwhile Messmer and his legal advisors concentrated on the lawsuit to the exclusion of all else. The case reached the state supreme court and to Messmer's relief the justices ruled that "recommending to the members what they should read under pain of expulsion from the church communion is within the jurisdiction of every pastor and prelate of every church which professes to leave such matters to the determination of its clergymen".[55]

Meanwhile the *Catholic Citizen* had been appearing regularly in Milwaukee. It passed as the "Irish" paper because the Germans subscribed to the *Excelsior* or the *Columbia*. With a view to establishing a "non-partisan" paper for the entire province, Messmer founded the *Catholic Herald* in 1922 and endowed it with the masthead "The Official Paper". On October 24, 1923, the Wisconsin Catholic Publishing Co. was incorporated and $100,000 worth of capital stock was offered at $10.00 per share. The clergy bought a good deal of stock, but soon an attempt was made to merge the new organ with the *Daily American Tribune* of Dubuque. This project died together with the proposed editor, Mr. Nicholas Gonner. The *Herald* failed to flourish and the *Citizen* failed to atrophy so on December 11, 1931, Archbishop Stritch asked the priests to cede their stock to the archdiocese to facilitate merging the *Herald* with the *Citizen*. The composite showed little affinity with either ancestor.

More difficult than maintaining newspapers was the task of financing the diocese. Many of Messmer's letters flailed pastors who did not submit financial reports. Others sent in such slovenly documents that, said the archbishop, a school boy would be ashamed of them. Judging from the numerous repetitions, he noticed little improvement. If Messmer tried lecturing, he did not omit threatening. In a circular letter of February 11, 1913, he decreed suspension for those who did not send in reports and he repeated this on several occasions such as December 18, 1914, February 2, 1918, and December 22, 1920.

---

[55] *Wisconsin Reports* (1916), vol. 162, pp. 565-568. The collection *Cases and Briefs* in the University of Wisconsin Law Library contains much information on the suit.

The finances themselves were frequently as bad as the bookkeeping. According to published diocesan statements, the total due the diocese in 1912 was $21,737; a year later it amounted to $25,506, and by February of 1916 the total stood at $32,094. Messmer again placed the blame squarely on the pastors because he suspected that they were phlegmatic about raising money which was destined to leave their parishes. Besides reckoning with this natural provincial feeling, Messmer remembered that the *Kuryer* incited the laity to refuse to pay dues if their wishes were not granted. Just how far this spirit of "striking" had spread none could tell.

Messmer faced two extraordinary problems in Milwaukee: namely, liquidating the half million dollar debt on St. Josaphat's Church and that on St. George's. Katzer, his predecessor, knew that something would have to be done about St. Josaphat's but his premature death spared him the task. Messmer procrastinated as long as he could, but by 1911 he had to take action to save the credit of the diocese and avert a nation wide scandal.[56] Franciscans consented to take over the parish and most of the debt, but the diocese assumed what in those days was a herculean burden—about $120,000. To raise this sum Messmer made a levy on all parishes of the diocese, payable within four years. Concurrently he suspended the annual collections for the African missions, the Indian and Negro missions, and the Catholic University. Along with the financial statistics several intangibles must be considered. Some poor parishes which barely eked out an existence had to finance the extravagance of another pastor. Secondly, because the Poles as recent immigrants were closely knit together, other racial groups felt a marked antipathy toward helping them. Faced with

---

[56] Circular letter, April 28, 1911. Of the debt, $40,000 was due to banks, $20,000 to well-to-do people, and the balance to the laboring class. A bankruptcy sale would have brought less than 20 cents on a dollar. The letter referred to the "maladministration of financial affairs" as well as "the present ferment and commotion against church authority among a large number of the Polish people." A circular letter of November 21, 1916, said the tax for St. Josaphat's was levied "with the explicit approval of the Holy See."

this situation, Messmer had to talk down all opposition and rule ruthlessly.

He told his constituents: "We can no longer say: Let St. Josaphat's see to it, it is their business. No, it has become the common cause of the whole diocese. Let none say: It is a Polish affair, let the Polish parishes help St. Josaphat. No, it is a Catholic affair, and every Catholic of the diocese, whatever his nationality, must feel that it concerns our common Catholic faith. Nor is it of any earthly use to ask how the sad condition was brought about or to blame the dead. This will not ease but harden the task before us. Nor, I may add, will it help the case to blame myself or the diocesan counsellors for having assumed part of St. Josaphat's debt. . . . I feel assured that for the love of God and the honor of the Holy Church, priests and people in every parish of the archdiocese, foremost in the Polish parishes, will generously assist in bearing their share towards a prompt payment of this debt."

Years rolled by but the funds did not roll in. Finally on November 21, 1916, he issued the most drastic letter of his career. He gave fifty-one delinquent parishes one month to settle their accounts. If they lacked cash, they had to get loans. Even several large Polish parishes were in arrears: St. Adalbert's owed $1623, St. Casimir's $1504, St. Cyril and St. Methodius $3784, and St. Mary Czestochowa $758. Non-compliance with the archbishop's mandate meant a partial interdict *ipso facto:*

"No High or Solemn Mass will be allowed in such church, nor any organ play or chanting, no baptisms and no marriages, which functions will have to be performed in the parsonage, not in the sacristy; funerals are also forbidden in the church; but the body may be blessed at the door or in the vestibule. Let it be understood that neither Christmas nor New Year's Day will be exempt from the effects of this interdict, and that any priest who should dare to break this interdict or allow other parties to do so, on any pretense or in any manner, will be *ipso facto* and *instanter* deprived of his faculties".

In the end Messmer could sit back and muse over his success but he could never forget the avalanche of vituperation which had inundated him.

By comparison St. George's Lithuanian parish, also in Milwaukee, presented a petty problem. None the less, the archbishop thought it impossible to appeal to the lay people at the very moment when they had just rescued St. Josaphat's. The founders' committee had estimated that it would have 300 families and this statement was endorsed by Father Szukalski in whose church the Lithuanians met for separate services. They bought property at Fifth and Lapham Street, but debt followed debt until the $8,000 property was encumbered with $20,000 and an annual interest charge of $1,000. A sort of post-mortem examination disclosed that only 72 families could be relied upon to support the parish so on February 1, 1916, Messmer asked his 300 priests for an average donation of $50.00 to avert bankruptcy. Within four weeks they pledged almost all of the amount and thereby placed the credit of the diocese beyond suspicion.

For the archdiocese the period before the war was hard, but the boom of the war years bettered the condition of the new and still struggling parishes. Institutions did not make as much progress and the seminary especially failed to prosper. In 1916 Messmer called attention to this during his address to the convention of the Catholic Knights of Wisconsin at Oshkosh. The seminary, he said, was no longer among the greatest in the country and the diocese had difficulty in defraying even its most basic expenses. Attentive to his plea, the Knights undertook to erect a gymnasium at St. Francis but their campaign was only partially successful. Consequently, early in the twenties the archbishop tried to capitalize on the lush times by launching a drive for $5,000,000 to renovate the seminary and the charitable institutions of the entire province. The details of the program he entrusted to the Ward System Co. of Chicago.[57] At the outset the bishops of Superior and

---

[57] William George Bruce, *I Was Born In America* (Milwaukee, 1937), pp. 385-387.

Marquette reneged because they were sponsoring other financial programs.[58] Next agents of the Ward Co. turned out to be plain spendthrifts, so in his distress the archbishop turned to a layman, William George Bruce, and pleaded with him to step into the breach. He did, and Messmer accorded him the rather rare privilege of speaking from the pulpit when he appealed for the institutions.

Judging from Messmer's correspondence, many priests gave little co-operation. One reason lay in the proposal to re-locate the theological department. This exasperated some loyal alumni who thought it quasi-sacrilegious to train priests anywhere else than in St. Francis. Secondly, Monsignor Breig, an affable but relatively unknown character, had recently become rector in place of saintly Monsignor Joseph Rainer who had spent a long lifetime promoting the welfare of the seminary. To dislodge the latter on account of his age probably required more courage than any other appointment in the archbishop's career, but many alumni felt that only one of their own number should succeed him. Others again regretted that Messmer put so foreign a type at the helm precisely when the seminary was Americanizing faster than ever before. Lastly, priests not of German descent often criticized the seminary for being a "closed corporation" even if it was the diocesan seminary. In the last analysis the drive was not a success even if it did provide funds for some very necessary improvements.

In purely ecclesiastical administration changes were few. Two years after Messmer's arrival in Milwaukee, that is in 1905, the Holy See created the diocese of Superior to develop the Church in northern Wisconsin. This diminished the diocese of Milwaukee slightly by allotting some parishes in southwestern Wisconsin to La Crosse and a change in the boundaries of Green Bay deprived Milwaukee of some parishes on its northern extremity. Previously rivers had formed the boundaries of the dioceses with the result that the north sides of Manitowoc and Oshkosh belonged to Green

---

[58]Circular letters, Aug. 26, 1920; Sept. 14, 1920.

Bay and the south sides to Milwaukee. The east sides of Wisconsin Rapids, Stevens Point, Wausau, and Merrill belonged to Green Bay and the west sides to La Crosse. Making county lines the diocesan boundaries neatly eliminated this confusion.

Not Messmer but Falconio, the apostolic delegate, consecrated Schinner as first ordinary of the new diocese. The appointment of Schinner disappointed the Poles. In 1903 they had hoped that one of their nationality would succeed Messmer in Green Bay. Next they looked for recognition in Superior. Again in vain. Schinner's promotion was somewhat noteworthy in that he had been close to Katzer whose proteges normally did not attain fame. In a long pastoral issued on February 8, 1912, this Benjamin in the hierarchy of Wisconsin dealt with immigration and nationalism in a way that would have wrung a "Bravo" from his old mentor.

Schinner attacked the slogan: Americanize the Church. He said that in other lands, it is alleged, the Church is decrepit but a new and glorious epoch will dawn if only she will accept American ideas. But Catholics must reject this passport to popularity because they cannot subscribe to the theory that the Church instead of teaching America must be her pupil. Such flattery of our neighbors approximates a denial of the divine prerogatives of the Church. Schinner then deprecated putting pressure on the immigrants and praised the superiority of European Catholics in the arts and sciences. He further dealt with the demand for more cardinals in the United States as well as with the weakness of the Catholic press and the shortcomings of some Catholic societies. Toward the end of his long letter he summarized:

"The Holy Ghost is not perfected by man, man is perfected by the Holy Ghost. From this it follows that the Church upon whom the Holy Ghost has been poured out and to whom the Holy Ghost was promised until the end of time, is not perfected by nationality or national characteristics, rather national characteristics are perfected by the Church. It is not through America that the Church shall find salvation. America shall find salvation through the Church."

Within the diocese of Milwaukee the most significant development was the appointment of an auxiliary bishop. The first of these was Bishop Koudelka, an American Bohemian who had been made bishop in 1907 with special jurisdiction over the Slavs in the diocese of Cleveland.[59] Never before had there been such an arrangement in the United States. With some irony this occurred in the diocese over which Gilmour, the determined opponent of Abbelen, had recently presided.

The appointment of Koudelka elicited some newspaper discussion to the effect that the Poles looked upon his coming with disfavor in view of the fact that they had 8,000 communicants with ten churches in contrast to the Bohemians with two churches and 1,000 members. Father Kruszka still believed the pope would honor their wishes even if it was unjust to give recognition to the Bohemians at an earlier date. According to him a German bishop would have been less objectionable than a Bohemian because the Germans were numerous. Kruszka's concept of the terms "auxiliary" and "archbishop" seems to have been hazy for he alleged that the former had not proved satisfactory and what was needed was "an archbishop with jurisdiction to settle all matters pertaining to the diocese".

After Koudelka served two years as pastor of St. Peter and St. Paul Church in Milwaukee he succeeded Schinner as bishop of Superior. His place was filled by Kozlowski. Messmer, assisted by Archbishop Weber and Bishop Richter, consecrated him on January 14, 1914. Although not universally popular, the Poles had in him the fulfillment of their wish for representation in the hierarchy of the province. He took up his residence at St. Stanislaus Church in Milwaukee amid rejoicing, but within a year his death turned joy into sorrow. The archbishop again administered the diocese by himself but the Poles enjoyed some compensation in the transfer of Bishop Rhode to Green Bay and into Messmer's province.

Despite Messmer's prestige as a metropolitan who ruled for over a quarter of a century he rarely had a chance to consecrate a

---

[59]Barry, *Church and German Americans*, p. 253.

bishop. Besides Kozlowski he consecrated Bishop Fox in 1904, in 1906 he went to Switzerland to consecrate Bishop Ruegg, a classmate of his, and in 1922 he consecrated Bishop Pinten. The controversy of Abbelen's days placed Milwaukee under a cloud that was slow to lift itself. Few Wisconsin priests became bishops, and when Messmer undertook to boost Muldoon—also a friend of the Federation—for Chicago his efforts ended in failure.

Foremost among Messmer's attempts to establish uniformity of discipline was the *Handbook for Catholic Parishioners* (1907), a book of 126 pages. Though based on the third plenary council of Baltimore, and not at all revolutionary, it contained prudent, interesting observations. Besides stating general principles on which the Church operates, it gave detailed information on administration. The first part emphasized the need for parishes incorporating and maintaining inventories. The salary of pastors fluctuated between $600 and $1000 pending the approval of the archbishop, and assistants received at least $300. This latter sum was to be paid them directly by the parish. Sunday collections constituted part of the pastor's salary, but he had the option of surrendering them in favor of a fixed sum. Pastors, however, had to furnish their own altar wine and altar breads and the lay trustees were to be compensated in some way for their service.

Messmer did not regard these regulations as giving a raise. On March 25, 1920, he wrote that there had been no general increase in salary for thirty years. Thereafter city pastors received $1,000 together with the Sunday, Christmas, and Easter collections. Those who forwent the collections received a minimum of $800 in recompense. A city was defined as a community with at least 10,000 inhabitants. Country pastors received $1,200 with collections and curates $500. For each of the latter the pastor could claim $400 board money.

The *Handbook* aimed at popularizing the views of Pius X on church music and it naturally endorsed Catholic education. In a democratic vein its author approved having a school board of laymen, headed by the pastor, to visit the school. He endorsed parish libraries but seems to have envisioned them as serving juveniles primarily. Conversely, he urged Catholics to keep an eye on the public libraries. The age for first Holy Communion throughout the province was set at twelve years. Catechism was to be taught in two languages where necessary. The opponents of this regulation he accused of laboring under "a lamentable ignorance of the needs of the Catholic Church in this country or a sinful and blind nationalism". It was his conviction that Catholics should influence politics for good, and he showed considerable hostility toward tavernkeepers because much parish wrangling originated at the bar. Regarding organized labor he epitomized his earlier remarks: "In our days many labor unions are, unfortunately, entirely committed to the false and pernicious principles of socialism."[60]

Besides making his own laws and promulgating them in the *Handbook* he scheduled a provincial council for August 18, 1908. Father O'Hearn would be the secretary and Father Becker the *magister cantorum*. The *schema* would run from six to eight chapters.[61] Four years later one of his circular letters on finance referred to an impending diocesan synod, but in 1915 this expert on councils let slip the defeatist observation "presuming that a diocesan synod is probably far off."

While waiting for such events to materialize he took issue with current abuses and promulgated new decrees from Rome. In 1908 he urged the clergy to explain the new laws of Pope Pius X respecting marriage and in 1911 he took up the perennial question of assistants. After making the unoffensive observation that the pastor-assistant relationship is not so clearly defined as in Europe, he proceeded to point out that mistakes are more likely to be made by the inexperienced clergy. Young men are the equals of the pastors in orders but in ecclesiastical position they stand in the relationship of inferior to superior. They are neither assistant rectors nor assistant pastors even though such titles may

---

[60]*Handbook*, p. 102.

[61]Messmer to Rainer, June 13, 1908, Bischofszell. Messmer had addressed the Katholikentag of St. Gallen. The letter directed Rainer to call the consultors together to prepare for the council. Ms. in the Salzmann Library, St. Francis, Wis.

be in current use. They merely serve the men to whom they are assigned. These have the right to regulate the order of the rectory and should know the whereabouts of the curates when they are gone. On the other hand, pastors should treat the young men with charity, forbearance, and fatherly affection. In the course of the letter he emphasized the necessity of teaching catechism: "It is unpardonable in both pastors and assistants to neglect these classes simply because some football or baseball is going on." After lamenting the waste of time that should have been devoted to theological and ascetic reading he again struck at this growing threat to the priestly character: "It is truly sad to be told that some young priests know a great deal more of various sports and sporting celebrities than of Catholic books and Catholic writers." While the letter professedly dealt with assistants it failed to canonize pastors whose conduct prompted him to caution curates that "the sin of my superior is no excuse for my own sin."

In 1913 Pope Pius X proclaimed the jubilee of the peace of Constantine. On August 27 Messmer forwarded the document to his priests together with some comments. Among these was a recommendation to provide penitents with a variety of confessors. He thought it well for priests to exchange confessionals the way ministers exchange pulpits because "it is a false principle and entirely opposed to the spirit of the Church to compel parishioners to go to their own pastor to confession", and regarding the condition of almsgiving he suggested that it could be fulfilled close to home by making a donation to the parish school.

Two years later he discouraged long range foundation Masses. No agreement should exceed twenty-five years. The sooner Masses are offered the better it is for the souls in purgatory. These, in turn, benefit more from a larger number of low Masses than from a smaller number of high Masses.

That same year, on October 9, 1915, he forwarded Pope Benedict XV's constitution authorizing three Masses on All Souls' Day. This new pope had from his early years cultivated devotion for the holy souls in purgatory. His stay in Spain as secretary to the papal nuncio brought him into close contact with the special privileges enjoyed there on November 2. Now that he was pope he extended them to the whole world. The archbishop hoped that his priests would utilize this new privilege and exhort their people to attend the Masses in large numbers. However he erred in stating: "From the tenor of the document it appears clearly enough that no choice is given of saying only two Masses; either all three must be said, or only one."[62]

By way of amplification Messmer added some of his own reflections. In contrast to the Holy Father who sympathized with the dead soldiers Messmer thought of those living ones who faced sudden death or their last agony. On them God had not yet passed the irrevocable judgment. "Is it not a far greater act of genuine Christian charity", he queried, "to save even one soul from the everlasting fire of hell, than free a thousand from the flames of purgatory?" Combining both ideas, he told his priests that they could weave a beautiful rosary of mementos by remembering at Mass first the soldiers who would fall in the next twenty-four hours and then those who had fallen in the last twenty-four hours.

Small wonder that he wanted his priests to join the diocesan purgatorial society which dated back to 1865. To those who were aggrieved at forgoing some stipends he wrote: "I hate the very thought that some mercenary motive might keep anyone from joining the society. What is the loss of a few paltry stipends for the Masses to be said compared with our spiritual gain here and hereafter? Nothing but *stercora.*" In order to facilitate administration, he recommended that St. Michael's Priest Fund and the purgatorial society be merged, but the proposal foundered.

Though Heiss had established deaneries long ago, they played a restricted role in the archdiocese. Messmer again carefully parcelled out the territory and after the new code appeared canon 131 received due attention. Just as Heiss had assigned topics for study Messmer designated a number of places as centers for conferences

---

[62]Decision No. 4342 of the Sacred Congregation of Rites, Feb. 28, 1917, did not uphold Messmer's view.

but the program quickly fell into desuetude. In 1924 he issued new faculties with the observation that Rome had withdrawn some privileges and that priests needed to study the new code.[63] Previous faculties, for example, had been generous in regard to reading and retaining forbidden books, they allowed the recitation of five decades of the rosary in place of the breviary in the event of sickness or *assidui laboris,* and three times a year priests could grant a plenary indulgence under the usual conditions.

On many occasions he exhorted priests to observe the rubrics and proper decorum. Their knowledge was to include solemn functions, and those who could not sing the Preface and Pater Noster respectably should not be invited to offer Mass at solemn occasions. "Personal regard must give away to the dignity of the divine service." His interest in church music led him to idolize Sir John Singenberger, the prolific composer who made the normal school at St. Francis the national center for church music. When the *Motu Proprio* of 1903 caused doubts about retaining women in choirs, it was Messmer who obtained a clarification of the matter from the Holy Father. This, in turn, was broadcast by the *Caecilia,* a periodical which Singenberger founded and edited for fifty years.[64]

This item contains two interesting remarks. First of all, Messmer disavowed anything like liturgical repristination: "While all three, discipline, worship, and music rest forever on the same unchangeable principles of Christ's doctrine and jurisdiction, which called them into existence in the beginning, yet the external forms of primitive Christianity, unless divinely ordained, will change and the letter of the primitive law give way to the spirit of later days. This applies to the liturgical music fully as much, if not more, as to anything else in the Church."

---

[63] In 1904 Gasparri invited the past and present professors of Canon Law at the Catholic University to take part in the proposed codification. Gibbons urged Messmer to participate but he was reluctant. Barry, *Catholic University,* p. 176.

[64] *Caecilia,* Feb., 1909, pp. 9-10. *Milwaukee Sentinel,* Sept. 27, 1904, gave Messmer's views on church music.

Secondly, regarding his own prerogatives, Messmer insisted: "It has always been a principle of canon law that bishops have the right to determine how and in what manner and to what extent some general law of the Church, which is after all a *lex humana* subject to the same rules and principles of interpretation and application as other laws emanating from human authority, shall be carried out in the actual, given circumstances and conditions of their dioceses and diverse parishes."

On May 1, 1911, he expressed a similar opinion in a pamphlet commenting on the Roman decree concerning the first Holy Communion of children. "The decree", he wrote, "embodies such a radical change from what had become a widespread custom in many parts of Europe and America that its real purpose and object was misunderstood by many who only read the dead letter without catching the living spirit. With an utter disregard of theological principle, of the spirit of former Church legislation, and of the common teaching of the theologians, some men rushed into print to discourse about the 'divine right' of little children to receive Holy Communion and about the 'divine law' binding parents and pastors to admit them, with no other result than to confuse the minds of the faithful, to frighten the conscience of pious priests and parents, and to disturb the uniformity of discipline. They were quite ready, as some one said, to force their own interpretation of the decree upon the bishops, forgetting that outside of the Holy See the bishops are the only authorized interpreters of the laws of the Church, and that it belongs to them alone to determine in what manner the law shall be carried out in their dioceses so as to accomplish its purpose. Hence our Holy Father, when asked by several bishops regarding this new decree and especially its ruling as to the age and instruction required for first Holy Communion, replied that it must be left to the conscientious judgment of the bishops themselves to decide according to the circumstances and the spiritual conditions prevailing in their dioceses. . . .

"The decree in no way decides how soon after the seventh year or at what age children actually do have the necessary discretion implying the knowledge and devotion becoming the Holy

Sacrament. It is here precisely where no fixed age can be assigned; it is here where the very theologians quoted in the decree, St. Thomas, Ledesma, Vasquez, St. Antoninus, to whom might be added St. Liguori, St. Charles Borromeo, Benedict XIV, De Lugo, Sanchez, nearly unanimously teach that while a child of seven years might possibly, in some very extraordinary case have sufficient discretion to receive Holy Communion yet children before the age of ten years rarely have such discretion, that others may not get it before they are twelve and even fourteen years old."

Messmer demanded piety as well as knowledge. Nor ought the former to be confounded with "mere sentimental gushing". "It is absolutely improbable that the Roman decree when speaking of seven years intended to set aside or condemn the common teaching of the greatest theologians in the Church. Its whole tenor is directed against the practice of putting off first Holy Communion until the twelfth year."

As a corollary to his arguments he laid down the law that thereafter children should be admitted to first Holy Communion at the age of ten. Exceptional children could be taken earlier. Throughout his pamphlet Messmer insisted on the need of catechetical instruction. While he conceded that American children may be brighter than those of Europe he countered with the observation that pastors, teachers, and even parents complain that their most difficult task is to interest these same children in Christian Doctrine.[65]

Respect for the sacraments prompted him to take a rigorous attitude toward feminine fashions. To him, for example, the "hiking suit", was "a most outrageous, downright immodest and positively sinful fashion", and "no decent girl with any sense of

---

[65] In a circular of Dec. 30, 1916, he reminded pastors that the diocesan rule was ten years. He was annoyed with those who admitted children at 8 or 9. When the American conditions were explained to Pius X he allowed the bishops of the province to observe the former rule of twelve years. Exceptions can be made but some priests place themselves above the bishops and follow "a policy which is based on a slavish interpretation of the pope's letter but has no solid theological ground to rest upon."

Christian modesty, decency, and propriety will ever go on the street in such an abominable 'hiking suit' ". Girls in such apparel were forbidden to enter a church, regardless of whether services were in progress or not, and no woman with a low cut dress reaching below the collar bone, or with bare arms, was allowed to receive Holy Communion.

At a time when few challenged feminism he charged his clergy to preach decency in dress and he warned that it was "time that the women begin to stop all those unnecessary expenses for dress and fashion that have in so many cases eaten up all the earnings of a hard working husband." On another occasion he took a stand against woman suffrage and published a pamphlet of thirty-six pages marshalling all the arguments he could find against this change in American politics. The pamphlet grew out of an address delivered in Watertown, Wis., to the State Federation of Catholic Societies. Although the *Milwaukee Sentinel* gave it provocative headlines, his remarks were temperate. He referred to "the infidel, unchristian character which to a great extent characterizes these modern women's movements. It started with the appearance of the French infidels and found its first expression in the French Revolution. It found its next endorsement in the socialistic platform published in 1848 and ever since it has been one of the great leading principles of socialism. . . . There may be no objection to granting women a certain modified suffrage. . . . A woman may do good work as a member of the school board when we would not want her for a representative at Washington. One corresponds to a woman's nature and the other does not. Woman is a natural educator, she understands the nature of children far better than do men."[66]

Likewise, in a letter of March 16, 1911, he took a vigorous stand against free schoolbooks. Just then such legislation was

---

[66]*Milwaukee Sentinel*, May 25, 1913. The speech elicited some comments from the readers. Messmer contributed a letter which appeared *ibid.*, May 29, 1913. The writer could not locate a copy of the pamphlet. *America*, July 31, 1915, p. 406, commented on it, and the *Bulletin of the American Federation of Catholic Societies*, Oct. 1914, quoted from it.

pending. He directed pastors and societies to arrange public meetings and send protests to their congressmen. To him the proposal suggested state paternalism and would lead to advanced socialism. Granted that "the state has direct and immediate interests in the education of its children", education is nevertheless first and foremost the duty of the parents and of the family. In Christian philosophy the family is above the state just as it precedes the state in the order of nature. Consequently, the state should not assume such duties as long as the parents fulfill them. Free books, free meals, and free transportation were all equally undesirable in his eyes.

Taking the cost of education at $36.46 per child he argued that Wisconsin Catholics saved the state $2,311,000 by maintaining their own grade schools. This figure did not include children in orphanages and students in advanced schools. He mentioned the educational efforts of the Lutherans and queried whether Catholics and Lutherans were "to be still more heavily taxed just in order to furnish the public schools with free textbooks." If so, they will be compelled to provide free books in their own schools to meet the competition.[67]

If Messmer warned Catholics to defend the independence and freedom of their schools from "any and all unjust and unnecessary state interference" he was not on principle averse to accepting public funds.[68] "Let the state examine our children and if our

---

[67] In the *Handbook*, p. 60, Messmer wrote: "School-money, if there must be such, should be as low as possible; it should not be collected by the teachers, whose dignity suffers by such practice. Let the parents, not the children, pay it directly to the secretary of the parish, unless a special collector be appointed for the purpose. The school books and stationery should be bought by the parish; but whether bought by the parish or the priest or sisters, they must be sold to the children for exactly the same price as bought from the publishers. For more than one reason it is poor policy to make up the teachers' salary by overcharging the children for books and stationery."

[68] In Messmer's opinion Catholic schools were not purely private enterprises. They were as public as any other schools and were genuinely schools of the people. *Bulletin of the Catholic Educational Association*, Nov., 1907, p. 22.

work is up to the standard required by the state, then in the name of all that is fair and just, let the state pay its share toward the support of our schools. If our work is not satisfactory, we shall not ask for the state compensation."

In 1920, when the Smith-Towner bill was pending, he mailed his priests a circular written by Rev. Jones Corrigan, S. J., listing ten reasons for defeating the bill. The latter stigmatized it as a step toward federal bureaucracy and ossified education which would tax the north to educate the south. It would flout the principle that education is basically local. Messmer, though urging societies to send protests to their congressmen, contented himself with one statement: "The 'Catholic' reason for its defeat lies in the fact that some of the provisions greatly menace our Catholic schools and their independence from state interference."

Midway between the two educational crises Messmer had to take a stand on World War I. The mobilizations found him in Europe, and only after a long delay did he get back to the United States. In those tense weeks he dropped a note to Father Traudt at the chancery office which immediately found its way into *Columbia:* "I pray for the victory of the just cause of Germany and Austria." At the time few readers sensed anything unusual in the archbishop's note, but soon he himself discerned that fewer people rhapsodized about the Monroe Doctrine and more and more repudiated isolationism. He never changed to the extent of advocating intervention but he did emphasize increasingly the duty of loyalty to one's country.

This was not done to gain prestige. The German element refused to be stampeded into believing the atrocity stories about the armies of Emperor William II and many of the Irish, rich in family lore, did not relish fighting for England. Nor did the allies beam promises of self determination to them as they did to the Poles who saw in Wilson's Fourteen Points the rebirth of their fatherland. Then, too, Wisconsin sent the first Socialist to the House of Representatives in the person of Victor Berger, a pacifist. Senator La Follette opposed the war and won a following that surpassed Berger's, while Milwaukee elected Mayor Hoan in 1918 on a platform that avowed: "The American people did not want and do not want this war. They were plagued into this abyss by the treachery of the ruling class of the country—its demagogic agitators, its bought press, its sensational photoplays, its lying advertisements, and other purchasable instruments of public expression."[69]

On October 25, 1916, Messmer forbade his priests under pain of *ipso facto* loss of faculties to participate in the Hughes-Wilson campaign.[70] To him this was only a repetition of the general legislation of the third council of Baltimore. The following month, however, he gave public evidence of not having forgotten the Austria that had assisted his diocese and had adopted him in his college days. When Emperor Francis Joseph died he led the priests who came from his empire in a memorial service in St. John's Cathedral. He himself offered the Mass and saintly Monsignor Rainer preached. The latter, known for his almost painful reticence, ventured to say: "Though I have severed political ties to enjoy the rights of an American citizen, my love and devotion to the imperial house of Austria and the venerable emperor can be torn from my heart by no earthly power, and no distance, however great. The citizen of a republic bows his head in respect when he beholds virtue and nobility of soul incarnate on a throne. . . . May this new king wear the double crown of Austria and Hungary with honor and rule long and peacefully over a united, undefeated Austria."[71]

As the war spread, Messmer repeated his requests for prayer. He encouraged women to join and form Red Cross circles, he endorsed the Junior Red Cross, he solicited aid for the military

---

[69]Robert C. Reinders, "Daniel W. Hoan and the Milwaukee Socialist Party During the First World War", *Wisconsin Magazine of History*, Autumn, 1952, p. 52.

[70]An incident at Marytown probably precipitated this letter. Rev. Edward Stehling started services late and preached long to keep his parishioners away from a Wilson rally. He urged the parish to pray to be delivered from another Wilson administration. *Milwaukee Journal*, Oct. 27, 1916.

[71]*Milwaukee Journal*, Nov. 30, 1916.

program of the Knights of Columbus, and he promoted the purchase of liberty bonds by all and war savings stamps by school children. On October 28, 1917, he issued a long, calm letter at a time when many leaders lost their equilibrium entirely. Its burden was: The government must be obeyed. Private judgment cannot appraise the rightness of the war. "In the congress", wrote Messmer, "lies the lawful and supreme authority of our nation. . . . Was congress justified in proclaiming this war. . . . ? Unless it could be shown by conclusive evidence, so as to convince the nation itself, that our representatives in congress were entirely mistaken in judging of the sufficient reasons for war, every citizen is bound to accept the judgment of the supreme authorities and must obey, willing or unwilling; but obey they must for conscience sake, for that is God's will."

Messmer maintained that neither the constitution nor Christian morality justifies a war to thrust liberty and democracy upon other nations. We may only protect or vindicate our national rights. On the other hand, Messmer hoped that "full political liberty" would come to the Irish, Poles, Lithuanians, and others. He further hoped for "full religious liberty" for France, Italy, and the Balkans as well as "full liberty and political independence" for the Holy Father who remained a prisoner in the Vatican ever since Italy had absorbed the papal state by force in 1870.[72] These, said the archbishop, can be secondary or concomitant objectives of the war. If industrialists make excessive profits, this does not release citizens from the duty of loyalty to their country. None the less citizens "have the right to demand of the government that it will use all its means and power to prevent any such unjust robbing of the money of the people and the nation. But even if it did not entirely succeed in doing so, this would not release us

---

[72]Benedict XV referred to the problem in his inaugural encyclical. The spread of the war emphasized the awkward position of the Holy See. Italy entered the war on condition that the pope be excluded from the peace conference. The pope appointed a committee of cardinals to study the problem. Gasparri announced that a solution was expected from a sense of justice rather than from force. Josef Schmidlin, *Papstgeschichte der Neuesten Zeit* (Munich, 1936), vol. III, pp. 258-264.

from our duty and loyalty as long as the cause of the nation is just."

American Catholics should continue to pray for the success of their army, but their prayers for the dead should include all soldiers regardless of their allegiance or nationality. Nor should they languish in praying for peace. "There is far more Christianity and consequently more patriotism in the fervent prayer for the glorious victory of an honorable peace than in the prayer for the cruel victory of bloody arms. The slogan: 'War to the finish under all conditions' is pagan, not Christian. When the guarantee of our rights can be obtained by peaceful negotiation, the justice of war disappears like the thinning clouds, and bloodshed becomes murder."

Incidental to the war hysteria was the regulation that after January 1, 1917, all parish records were to be kept in English or at least in both languages. No person was thereafter eligible for trusteeship if he could not read and write English. On February 2, 1918, the archbishop again praised the Junior Red Cross and the children's War Savings Stamps Campaign. Descending to a practical level he cautioned "that the Catholic clergy cannot afford, especially at this time of the war excitement, to show any apathy or disaffection in these legitimate patriotic movements. If it were for no higher motives, the temporal interests of the Church alone compel us to help the good will of the whole American people and its authorities. Nor can we allow the impression to go out, right or wrong, that the public schools are the only schools where true patriotism and loyal duty to the country are being cultivated."

Besides the European embroglio there was a lesser one in Mexico. After Diaz at long last left office in 1911 Madero succeeded him. He was, in turn, assassinated a few days before Wilson took office. The latter refused to recognize Huerta on the grounds that "just government rests upon the consent of the governed". The Niagara Falls Conference averted war, and Huerta fled the country, but Carranza, whom the United States immediately recognized, promptly began harassing the Church.

Father Francis Kelley, the editor of *Extension,* for one, wrote forcefully about the matter. Messmer, seconded by his suffragans, asked Gibbons on December 23, 1914, whether the three American cardinals would deem it advisable to issue "a solemn protest against the Mexican outrages upon the Catholic priests and religious." His Eminence disagreed with Kelley and advised Messmer on December 26 that it would be useless to address the lawless rulers of Mexico. Nor did he favor sending a protest to Washington. Wilson probably saw clearly the folly of not recognizing Huerta and was doing all he could to rectify the mistake. When Gibbons consulted Ireland the latter sputtered that the Wisconsin bishops were "fussy" people "unconscious of American public opinion—ready to embroil the Church into difficulties of any and every kind".[73] Ireland continued: "A letter of the three cardinals is rather a too solemn document to be put forth without pressing need and without assurance of success. Besides, apart from your own name, the document would have no weight with the country. Archbishop Keane of Dubuque is here while I write and says the document should not be thought of." The matter rested there, but on January 26, 1917, Pope Benedict XV broke all precedents and embarrassed the experts on diplomacy in Washington by cabling an appeal on behalf of the Mexican bishops directly to Wilson.

Despite their irreconcilable differences in outlook, the feelings between the archbishops of St. Paul and Milwaukee were not uninterruptedly tense. In 1911 when Ireland celebrated his golden jubilee Messmer wrote to him with some candor distilled with diplomacy:

"Permit me on this occasion to say how sorely disappointed I was at the news that the dignity of cardinal had not been bestowed upon you. I make no secret of my deep regret and I am glad to say that in these sentiments I am not the only one among German American bishops in the U.S. Bishop Fox of Green Bay

---

[73]Mss. in the archives of the Baltimore archdiocese. Bishop Schrembs made an issue of the Mexican persecution in his sermon before the Federation of Catholic Societies on Sept. 27, 1914.

was quite strong in his expressions. . . . I, for one, will hope for the happy event in the not far future."[74]

If the advisability of intervening in Mexico put the neighboring archbishops in opposite camps, the desirability of making the United States dry likewise found them poles apart. Prohibition won no commendation from Messmer. A dozen years before the country went dry he had denounced drunkenness and the abuses connected with saloons. He wanted earnest Christians to "concentrate their forces on the enactment of laws for strict police supervision and control over the saloon and the sale of intoxicating liquors" but he did not think it necessary to resort to prohibition.[75] As this neo-Manichaeism gained disciples Messmer said that he saw "a strong sectarian power" back of the movement. Despite the fact that some priests participated in the movement in good faith, he himself sensed an attack on the Church in her most sacred mystery. On June 17, 1918, Messmer forbade pastors to allow prohibition speeches on church property yet he encouraged them to preach on temperance. "Prohibition", said he, "is in no sense moderation, yet this is the true meaning of the cardinal virtue of temperance."

After the "noble experiment" got under way he warned his priests not to abuse the trust which the government placed in their requisitions for altar wine. As for himself, he no longer expected to be served alcoholic beverages on his official visits. Some years later, when criticism of the law mounted, he followed the lead of Cardinal O'Connell and Archbishop Hayes and expressed himself vigorously in an interview with the *Milwaukee Journal*.[76] Although he did not want prohibition to be a pulpit topic in his diocese, priests could discuss the matter before parish

---

[74]Barry, *Church and German Americans,* p. 271. Messmer had changed his mind with the passing of years. On Feb. 7, 1893, he wrote to Corrigan that Ireland ought not to get the red hat because "everybody would naturally consider it as an authoritative endorsement of Archbishop Ireland's policy". Moynihan, *op. cit.,* p. 356.

[75]*Handbook,* p. 107.

[76]Feb. 13, 1926.

societies, and Messmer expected the laity to express themselves in the next congressional elections.

The archbishop characterized the eighteenth amendment as a police regulation. The framers of the constitution, however, never intended to fashion an instrument for the police to wield. By then the advocates of the law knew that it was a failure and there was only one remedy—repeal. Messmer assured the reporter that he did not advocate "disobedience to the Volstead law or any phase of the eighteenth amendment", but he expected public opinion to "manifest itself at the right time and with sufficient force."

"I may say frankly", reads the interview, "that I believe if light wines and beer were allowed there would be no more of this 'moon' liquor or home brews that tend to weaken sound physical bodies and make cowards of millions of people. The American people were never intemperate; they have always believed in freedom of thought and action consistent with decency and have conducted themselves accordingly.

"Drunkenness existing at the time the national prohibition law was enacted was far less than exists now and if the United States had spent half as much money then in enforcing laws as it now does in its delirious attempt to enforce the Volstead law there would have been no occasion for the eighteenth amendment."

If Messmer repudiated prohibition as a means of reforming human beings individually, still more vigorously did he reject socialism as a means of remaking society as a whole.

The lineage of Wisconsin socialism reaches back to the refugees of 1848 but it was Victor Berger, an Austrian immigrant, who established it firmly in Milwaukee. After teaching in the public schools he edited the *Wisconsin Vorwaerts* and presumably influenced Debs. Berger, however, did not idolize Marx. If he wanted saints he preferred "to join the Roman Catholic Church and get them wholesale". After Branch No. I of Social Democracy had been founded in Milwaukee in 1897 he strove to make socialism the political arm of trade unionism. Messmer, therefore, was well advised when early in his career he repeatedly censured labor unions because of their socialist tendencies.

The Socialists concentrated on city politics. Starting at the turn of the century as a nuisance party on the ballot they gained strength from election to election. Their aldermen began to influence the council, and in 1904 five Socialists were elected to the assembly and one to the senate. Five years later Berger's wife and Frederick Heath captured positions on the school board. The Socialists, always champions of the public schools, demanded free textbooks. Messmer, of course, opposed their demand with equal determination. Finally, in 1910 Berger was elected to the House of Representatives and Emil Seidel won the mayoralty by a comfortable majority.

For more than a decade David Rose, a Democrat, had given the stiffest opposition to any candidate for mayor. Many Polish priests were his partisans, but Messmer disapproved using church property for political purposes. By 1910, however, the Socialists controlled entire Polish and Catholic areas. This was especially noteworthy because Milwaukee Socialism was a German movement even if it boasted of its American character. The tactic of the Socialists was to win votes en bloc along national lines yet they forgot their leveling humanitarianism to the extent of ignoring the Negroes, and Berger discounted the importance of women because they were too reactionary and too subservient to the Church.

The archbishop, alert to the zeal of the reds, opposed them personally and through others. Father Dietz, for example, tirelessly exposed their fallacies. Father Sherman did so with almost unbecoming vehemence, Judge Carpenter crusaded as a layman, and *Columbia* tried to enlighten its readers through its columns. None the less, socialism remained strong up to World War I and during the war Daniel Hoan won the mayoralty on a defiant antiwar platform.

After the war Messmer warned his priests that the Socialists were trying to carry the elections of judges and members of the school board. His priests were to advise people to vote the nonpartisan ticket. He took the occasion to point out that social reform is not socialism. Public welfare projects have other origins. Too many Christians saw in socialism nothing more than a purely economic program designed to help the laboring class. Fearing that the women's vote would help the Socialists owing to the humanitarianism in their platform, the archbishop urged Catholic women to go to the polls regardless of what they personally thought of woman suffrage.

Messmer's detailed letter on socialism is extremely scholarly but its literary style points to another author. Maintaining that the Church fights socialism not as a political party but as a self-confessed enemy of Christianity, he contrasted Christianity with socialism and concluded with the warning:

"Do not say that here in America socialism will not be able to carry out its nefarious and anti-Christian principles in our public and national life. Europe today teaches us a terrible lesson. What socialism can and will do if given a free hand, stands clearly before us in the horrible deeds of the Bolsheviki. Bolshevism is not something new, though the name is new. Bolshevism is nothing else but the logical and absolutely necessary outcome of socialism wherever this system gets control of the public power and resources. Unless Americans fight socialism under every form and on every field, we shall infallibly have Bolshevism in our own beloved land before the present generation shall have passed. But a few years ago, who would have imagined that events and conditions as we see them in Europe today, would ever be possible?"

Autumn after autumn Messmer paid special attention to Thanksgiving Day. Frequently he sent out a circular letter on the subject. Besides recommending special prayers, he maintained that such a holiday could be an antidote to socialism. On November 17, 1914, for example, he wrote: "We all know of the tremendous and persevering endeavors of socialism and infidelity to establish modern society on the basis of unsectarian or neutral morality, independent and free from all religious principles. This insidious theory is spread broadcast among our laboring classes and a fertile soil for its rapid growth is prepared in the minds of the children of the land, unconsciously perhaps, yet none the less efficaciously, by the unsectarian principle of our public school.

Hence it becomes a sacred duty of our Catholic clergy to profit by such an opportune occasion as presented by a national thanksgiving day in order to bring home to our flock the old truth that the great teachings and principles of the Christian religion must guide and rule Christian citizens not only in their private conduct, but also in their public and civic life and thus pervade the social and national life of the country if our people are to enjoy true happiness and lasting peace."

Being archbishop in one of the nation's socialist strongholds[77] was not exceedingly unpleasant, yet he could never forget his duty to combat Marxism nor could he gauge accurately how successful the 'boring from within' was. This technique of compromise was Berger's forte yet it must be said that the latter denied being a Communist and he did draw distinctions between socialism and communism. Doubtless many people followed him primarily because no other reform movement offered any real hope of success. After World War I ended most people recognized that the Socialist party was moribund, and those who had sought salvation from it shifted their allegiance to various Progressives. These in many instances pirated their ideas from earlier leftists.

Since the Socialists stood ever ready to impale capitalists for corrupting morals they crusaded — often successfully — against graft, prostitution, drunkenness and the like. In Milwaukee the last was not always obvious because the Socialists often met in taverns and they recruited many members among the brewery workers. Among the outgrowths of this reform spirit was opposition to gambling. With aleatory games the warp and woof

---

[77] The progress of socialism in the county manifested itself in the presidential elections.

In 1900	Debs	polled	4,874	or	7% of the votes
1904	Debs		18,340		26%
1908	Debs		17,496		23%
1912	Debs		19,243		27%
1916	Benson		16,943		21%
1920	Debs		42,914		30%

of parish picnics, Messmer had to call attention to the anti-gambling agitation in 1921, and, as is well known, this matter still occasions considerable local friction between church and state.

Although Messmer ruled Milwaukee over a quarter of a century, his regime does not belong to the missionary epoch. It must be characterized as transitional. First of all, World War I made immigration impossible. Next legislation reduced it to small proportions. As a result, America became less a league of nations and more conscious of its own nationality. Bi-lingual schools, foreign language publications, and national parishes had to change or perish. The Germans were now "old immigrants", so their racial distinctiveness had been diluted, but on the other hand Messmer had to care for recent arrivals such as Slovenes, Slovaks, Croatians, Italians, and Hungarians, as well as Catholics of oriental rites. This meant finding foreign priests who were not readily available and multiplying churches for people who could hardly support them. Simultaneously Messmer plunged into the work of converting the Negroes. With the aid of the Capuchins he established St. Benedict the Moor Church and school in downtown Milwaukee and did monumental work at a time when few Catholics thought along such idealistic lines.

Institutional development came automatically in this era of transition. Hospitals, for example, sprang up everywhere and Messmer took an active part in the Catholic Hospital Association. His predecessors had won the battle for grade schools before his arrival but he standardized them by appointing Father Barbian diocesan superintendent of schools. Catholic high school education received scant consideration before the twentieth century. Yet by the time Messmer died it had become common. Rather fittingly a large Catholic co-educational high school bears his name. Being regional rather than parochial it reflects the conviction which he expressed to the Catholic Educational Association in 1911. "It is certainly a great mistake", said Messmer, "to have too many high schools in a limited space in neighboring parishes. There ought to be a system devised, or at least we ought to come to some general agreement that in cities the parishes will combine in maintaining a high school."[78]

If Messmer prized school work highly, he did not overlook those who lacked educational opportunities. In 1916 he founded the Catholic Instruction League to teach Christian Doctrine and American citizenship to youths and adults who needed such training. Secondarily the League offered wholesome recreation as a safeguard for the morals of the young people. In many instances the League climaxed its work by enrolling its clients in parochial schools.

The archbishop warmly endorsed societies in his *Handbook*. Among them he mentioned the society of St. Vincent de Paul. Although inactive in Milwaukee for fully thirty years it revived in 1908. Five years later a concerted effort was made to spread the society throughout the city and the local conferences were then federated into the particular council. Operating out of a central office this council provided spiritual ministrations for the inmates of public penal and welfare institutions. Through the St. Vincent de Paul Society, which enjoyed the advice of Haas and Muench, the diocesan charities were in a way co-ordinated. New — one might almost say premature — projects were launched such as a camp for boys, St. Charles Home for wayward boys, St. Margaret's Guild for neglected girls, and St. Bernard's Home for workingmen and transients.[79]

---

[78] *America*, Oct. 25, 1952, p. 93.

[79] Daniel T. McColgan, *A Century of Charity The First One Hundred Years of the Society of St. Vincent de Paul in the United States* (Milwaukee, 1951), vol. II, pp. 117-128; Albert P. Schimberg, *Humble Harvest The Society of St. Vincent de Paul in the Milwaukee Archdiocese 1849-1949* (Milwaukee, 1949).

Messmer in his *Handbook*, p. 100, summarized the teaching of the Church respecting secret societies. In minor matters he was not so strict as Katzer. He agreed with Archbishop Farley's comment: "If children want to have an innocent play, let them have it." *Proceedings of the Tenth Biennial Council Catholic Knights of Wisconsin* (Oshkosh, 1904), pp. 78-89.

He also promoted the Holy Name Society and authorized the Vincentians to address Holy Name meetings on the subject of charity. He was on friendly terms with the Knights of Columbus, especially the Catholic Interest Committee, and as early as 1907 he endorsed the Church Extension Society.

Much as he was interested in charities he did not support them out of a central treasury. He levied a tax for the orphans but for the rest he relied upon the thrift and ingenuity of the officers. Self reliance and personal contacts rather than bureaucracy appealed to him as a Swiss and as an immigrant who knew only the older, more individualistic economy. Belonging as he did to the era of transition, this outlook spared him many collisions with groups whose outlooks did not embrace the entire diocese, and the growth of institutions such as St. John's School for the deaf proved that the method was feasible.

Alongside of the works of charity mention must be made of the many religious communities which settled in the diocese. A few have assumed parish work while the others pursue their special objectives. Their mere presence, however, reflects Messmer's appreciation of the religious life.

Throughout his entire career Archbishop Messmer remained democratic. His full beard made him a marked man, yet he rode the street car without feeling ill at ease and he liked to take long walks unencumbered by members of his official entourage. At times he got away from his staid surroundings by visiting the Capuchins at Marathon, in northern Wisconsin, where he donned old clothes, helped clear the land and burn the underbrush. One day while taking a hike in old clothes he dallied to watch some farmers husk corn. Irked by the sight of a sturdy vagrant rich in leisure they offered him a job at fifteen cents a bushel. The oldster accepted. After finishing four bushels he suggested a glass of milk and some bread instead of cash. The farmer agreed and told him to come back whenever he felt like husking. Some time later a surprised farmer received an autographed picture of his "migrant worker" — the archbishop of Milwaukee.[80]

---

[80]Bittle, *op. cit.*, p. 465.

Though the archdiocese purchased the majestic Pabst residence for him, his tastes remained simple. Pomp was foreign to him, and he neither sought nor enjoyed the adulation in which high society abounds. A guttural "Bah" could well epitomize his comment on glamor. Garments like the *cappa magna* annoyed him. He preferred to keep ceremonies simple but correct. Somewhat rugged and brusque by nature, he was not given to toadying. So much so was this the case that when traveling he preferred to stay in a hotel rather than receive hospitality from a fellow bishop. Sad to say, his own dislike of obsequiousness made it hard for him to detect it in others who stooped to such tactics for self advancement.

When the golden jubilee of his ordination approached in 1921 his thoughts gravitated more and more to his parental home. So in a retrospective mood he went to Goldach to commemorate the event, and during his absence Father Traudt, the administrator of the diocese, organized a celebration for October in Milwaukee at St. John's Cathedral.

In the spring of 1924 he buried his close friend and the most decorated member of his diocese, Sir John Singenberger. That autumn another news dispatch startled Catholic America. This time it came from Washington. The archbishop took sick while attending the annual bishops' meeting. His ailment puzzled the physicians but there was reason for concern because his kidneys failed to function properly. However, it did not take long before he was back in Milwaukee.

Three years later his eightieth birthday occurred. Again he could think of nothing more attractive than to go to Switzerland where he could relax and entertain his friends and relatives at the "Rietli". At the sivler jubilee of his promotion to Milwaukee the diocese again rallied around him fully aware of the fact that age was furrowing his features and filching agility from his step. Repeatedly he received Extreme Unction but the news of imminent death from angina pectoris was invariably followed by the announcement that he had rallied. To the surprise of many, he lived to see the stock market crash and topple the prosperity of the twenties but Divine Providence spared him experiencing the depression. Late in May of 1930, as times were getting harder, fire destroyed historic St. Aemilian's Orphanage. He came to St. Francis to inspect the ruins and on June 14 he again came to St. Francis, this time to confer both minor and major orders in the seminary chapel. Shortly after that he and Monsignor Breig, who crossed the ocean with him seven times, left for Europe.

Under date of June 23 he sent out his last letter, obviously redacted by his staff, thanking his constituents for their prayers and asking that they be continued. He thanked the clergy for their donation on the occasion of his silver jubilee as archbishop and went on to exhort priests to arouse in their parishioners a high esteem for the sacrament of Confirmation "which has become of such tremendous importance in our days when the spirit of the world, of infidelity and immorality, is doing its very best to lead modern society away from God and His holy laws."

En route to Europe the archbishop called on Archbishop Fumasoni-Biondi, the apostolic delegate, and on June 29 he and Breig docked in Naples. After visiting Rome they went to his native village. There on August 4 his life cycle, extensive in time and space, closed symmetrically where it had begun. His companion deposited the worn body of his friend in the Swiss soil which he loved. It rests there in the gentle shadow of the trim little church at Goldach from which he quietly set out to follow the beck of the Divine Master, first to neighboring Austria to the altar, and then across the Atlantic to become a professor and an author in the east — a bishop and an archbishop in the west. A simple, sombre slab says nothing about this odyssey but soberly and hopefully announces: *Hier harrt seiner glueckseligen Auferstehung Seine Excellenz Dr. Sebastian Messmer Erzbischof von Milwaukee.*

INDEX

Abbelen, Rev. Peter M., 15 n., 38-39, 42, 43, 79, 124, 125
Absolution, 13, 28, 70
Abstinence, Total, 41, 42, 99. See also Prohibition.
Ad limina visits, 49, 69
Aemiliana, Mother, 16 n.
Age for First Holy Communion, 126, 130
Albertus Magnus Verein, 48
Alexandria, 72
All Souls' Day, 127-128
American Catholic Clerical Union, 39, 58
American Catholic Quarterly Review, 36, 66
American College, Rome, 87, 104, 107
American Conference of Catholic Trade Unionists, 112
American Ecclesiastical Review, 69, 85, 99
American Federation of Catholic Societies. See Federation of Catholic Societies.
American Federation of Labor, 112
Americanism, 75, 76-78, 104
Amherst College, 82
Anarchists, 101, 105 n.
Anima College, 46 n., 50, 107
Antigo Republican, 55 n.
A. P. A., 43, 55, 75, 105
Apollinaris College, 85
Apostacy, 12, 36-37, 60, 93
Apostolic Delegate, 24, 148. See also Satolli, Falconio, Fumasoni-Biondi
Appleton, 88, 101
Appleton Post, 98
Archbishops, Meetings of, 57, 65, 68, 69, 78, 100
Ashland, 23 n.
Assistants, 33, 125, 126
Australia, 47

Austria, 19, 46, 49, 72, 81, 83, 112, 134, 135, 148
Austro-Prussian War, 62
Authority of Church and bishops, 117, 130
Auxiliary bishops, 124

Balkans, 136
Baltes, Bishop Peter J., 66
Baltimore
    Council of 1849, 13, 20
    First plenary council of, 12 n.
    Second plenary council of, 20, 24 n., 41, 66
    Third plenary council of, 29, 30, 32, 34, 35, 37, 38, 42, 49, 63, 67, 71, 75, 84, 90, 91, 94, 95, 107, 125, 135
Banns of marriage, 28
Baraga, Bishop Frederick, 46, 47
Barbian, Rev. Joseph, 144
Bardstown, 11 n.
Barton, 81 n.
Batz, Rev. Leonard, 15, 16, 29
Baumgartner, Rosa, 82
Bavaria, 9, 14, 17, 19, 20, 21, 43, 48
Bayfield, 23 n.
Bayley, Bishop James R., 82, 83
Becker, Rev. Charles, 126
Belgians, 59, 89
Belgium, 62
Belle, Rev. Arthur, 50
Benedict XV, Pope, 127, 136 n., 138
Benedictines, 23, 32
Bennett, Michael John, 42 n.
Bennett Law, 42-44, 51-57, 58, 59, 60, 65, 72, 94, 96, 97
Berger, Victor, 134, 140, 141
Berger, Mrs. Victor, 141
Beurberg, 17
Bible Knowledge, Outlines of, 110
Bimetallism, 74
Bishop, Authority of, 117, 130
Black Legend, The, 75

Boeswald, Rev. Karl, 9, 10, 12, 12 n.
Bohemians, 22, 59, 124
Bolsheviki, 142
Bouquillon, Rev. Thomas, 64, 65, 72, 86
Boycott suit, 117
Breen, Rev. Andrew E., 110-111
Breig, Msgr. Augustine C., 122, 148
Breviary, 129
Brownson, Henry F., 70 n.
Bruce, William George, 122
Bruehl, Rev. Charles, 113
Bruell, Andrew, 110
Bryan, William Jennings, 74
Buchanan, James, 17
Bucharest, 72, 82 n.
Buffalo, N. Y., 14 n., 32 n., 48
Buffalo Mission of Jesuits, 41
Buh, Rev. Joseph, 46
Burial, Christian, 69
Burlington, 13

Caecilia, 129
Caecilia Society, 33, 129
Caecus Videns, 19
Cahensly, Peter Paul, 36, 60, 61, 88, 89, 92-94, 99, 111
Camberg, 72
Canonical Procedure in Disciplinary and Criminal Cases, 84
Canon Law, New Code of, 129
Capitalists, 34
Cappa magna, 147
Capuchins, 23, 72, 84, 144, 146
Carbonari, 68, 69
Card games, 113
Cardinalate for Abp. Ireland, 81
Cardinals, Demand for more, 123
Carolina Augusta, Empress, 46
Carpenter, Judge, 141
Carranza, Venustiano, 137
Carroll, Bishop John, 36
Catechism, 13, 33, 126, 127, 131
Cathedraticum, 28, 29
Catholic Church Extension Society, 146
Catholic Citizen, 69, 98, 118
Catholic Colonization Society, 100

Catholic Congress, 44, 98
Catholic Educational Association, 109, 144
Catholic Encyclopedia, The, 110
Catholic Herald, The, 118
Catholic high schools, 106, 144-145
Catholic Historical Review, 110
Catholic Hospital Association, 144
Catholic Instruction League, 145
Catholic Interest Committee, 146
Catholic Knights of Wisconsin, 106, 121
Catholic newspapers, 77, 92, 94, 95, 107, 114
Catholic Normal School, 19, 29, 33, 35, 48, 129
Catholic Register, 42 n.
Catholic Review of New York, 40
Catholic Social Welfare Bureau, 114
Catholic Students Mission Crusade, 113
Catholic Summer School, 102-104
Catholic Temperance League, 99
Catholic Total Abstinence News, 42
Catholic Total Abstinence Union, 99
Catholic University of America, 34-36, 39, 40, 44, 65, 79, 85, 86, 87, 103, 107, 108, 109, 110, 113, 119
Catholic workingmen's unions, 105, 106 n.
Centenary of American hierarchy, 43
Center Party, 105
Central Verein, 40, 51, 55 n., 75, 100, 104, 105, 106, 112, 113
Ceylon, 88
Chancery office, 29
Chicago *New World*, 90
Child labor, 43
Child, Rights of, 53, 130
Chilton, 88
Cholera, 14
Christian Apologetics, 110
Christian Brothers, 23
Christian Democracy, Encyclical on, 105
Church goods, 79
Church music, 19, 31, 101 n., 129

INDEX

Cincinnati, 12, 37, 41
Citizenship, U. S., 22
Civil War, 17
Cleary, Rev. James M., 42
Clergy conferences, 128
Clergy, Needy.
  See Priests, Support of
Clerical Society of Mary, 19
Clerical unions, 40, 86
Cleveland, Grover, 73
Cleveland, Ohio, 124
Coadjutor to Henni, 24-28, 35, 41, 58, 61
Coat of arms, Katzer's, 49
Colgosz, Leon, 101
Collections, 33, 125
Collections suspended, 119
Colleges, Secular, 109
Cologne, 72
Colonies, Catholic rural, 99-100
Columbia, 17, 26, 118, 141
Columbus, Ohio, 37
Commonwealth, Fond du Lac, 55 n.
Communism, 97
Compulsory Education, 43, 55 n., 56, 57
Concordat, Austro-Hungarian, 62
Confederates, 94
Confession, 70, 127
Confirmation, 148
Confraternity of Christian Doctrine, 109
Congress, U. S., 136
Constantine, Peace of, 127
Constitution, U. S., 18, 136, 140
Consultors, Diocesan, 59
Conversions, 12
Cornell University, 109
Corn husking, 146
Corrigan, Rev. Jones, 133
Corrigan, Abp. Michael A., 57, 78, 82, 85, 87, 88, 94, 139 n.
Covington, 11, 12, 12 n., 84
Curates. See Assistants
Czech, Mr., 50

Daily American Tribune, 118
Daily Northwestern, Oshkosh, 96

Dakota, Vicariate of, 32, 87
Damian, St. Peter, 17
Dance halls, 97
Deaneries, 128
Debs, Eugene, 140, 144 n.
Debts, 27 n., 28, 30, 119-121
Decree, Papal on First Holy Communion, 130-131
De Kelver, Rev. W., 55 n.
Delassus, Henry, 70 n.
Democratic Party, 18, 51, 55, 57, 73
Dempsey, Rev. Thomas, 42 n.
De Pere, 98
Depression
  of 1893, 71, 73, 74
  of 1929, 148
Deuster, P. V., 18
Devivier, Rev. W., 110
Devotions, 33, 39
Diaz, Porfirio, 137
Dietz, Rev. Peter E., 109 n., 112-113, 114, 141
Diplomacy of Benedict XV's note, 138
Dispensations, 28, 33
Ditramzell, 14
Divine Savior, Sisters of, 73
Divine Savior, Society of, 73
Doellinger, John, 16
Dominican Sisters from Regensburg, 16 n.
Doppelbauer, Bishop Francis, 46, 50, 72, 73 n., 79
Downing, Margaret B., 66
Draft in Civil War, 18
Drexel, Catherine, 79
Drive for institutions, 121
Droste, Rev. Francis, 84
Durward, Bernard, 15, 110
Dutch Catholics, 59
Dwenger, Bishop Joseph, 32 n., 37

Ebensee, 46, 50, 72
Edelbrock, Abbot Alexius, 32
Education, Catholic. See Bennett Law, Catholic University, Parochial Schools.

Education, To Whom Does It Belong?, 64
Egan, Maurice F., 103
Eichstaett, 9, 10, 11, 12 n., 15 n., 45 n.
Eighteenth Amendment, 139-140
Eis, Bishop Frederick, 71 n.
Elder, Abp. William H., 61
Elections, 134, 139, 140, 141
England, 134
England, Bishop John, 110
English language, 15 n., 22 n., 33, 42 n., 43, 53, 94, 137
English speaking bishops and priests, 39-40, 55 n., 57, 71 n., 87
English speaking Catholics, 22, 39, 59, 60,
Enzlberger, Rev. John, 31 n.
Episcopalian diocese of Fond du Lac, 88-89
Ernst, Dr., 10, 11
Escanaba, 55
Europa oder die Christenheit, 41
Evolution of man, 103
Excelsior, 118
Excommunication, 68-69
Extension, 138. See also Catholic Church Extension Society.

Faculties, 33, 129
Fagan, Rev. Thomas, 26
Fairbanks, Rev. H. F., 26
Falconio, Abp. Diomede, 80, 123
Family, The, 52, 100, 133
Faribault system, 63-65, 88, 91
Farley, Abp. John, 145 n.
Farmers, 100-101
Farrell, Rev. John, 109
Fashions, Feminine, 131-132
Federation of Catholic Societies, 104-107, 112-113, 115, 125, 132, 138 n.
Felker, C. W., 56 n.
Fenian Brotherhood, 66
Finances of Milwaukee archdiocese, 29, 43, 71, 118-122
First Holy Communion, 126, 130
Fitzpatrick, Rev. E. J., 26

Flag on Cathedral, 18
Flaget, Bishop Benedict, 11, 11 n., 12 n.
Flasch, Bishop Kilian C., 27, 32, 43, 44, 48, 51, 57
Flemish Belgian Catholics, 59
Foley, Bishop John S., 72
Fond du Lac, Wis., 80
Fond du Lac, Episcopalian Diocese of, 89
Fond du Lac *Commonwealth*, 55 n.
Foundation Masses, 127
Fox, Bishop Joseph J., 125, 138
France, 81, 136
Francis I, Emperor, 46
Francis Joseph, Emperor, 19, 46, 47 n., 72, 135
Franciscan Fathers, 23, 119
Franciscan Sisters of Perpetual Adoration, 16 n. See also St. Francis Convent.
Fransoni, Luigi Card., 68
Freemasons, 34, 54-55, 66-70
Free school books, 132-133, 141
Frei, Gertrude, 9
Freinberg, 46, 47, 48, 49, 72
French language and people, 22, 59
French Revolution, 11 n., 95, 97, 132
French speaking Catholics, 59
Fumasoni-Biondi, Abp. Peter, 148

Gabriel, Father, 84
Gambling, 143
G. A. R., 69
Gasparri, Peter Card., 129 n., 136 n.
Gavantus, 84
Georgianum, 9, 10
German bishops, 40-41, 56 n., 117
German Catholics 9, 11, 12, 13, 18, 22, 25, 32, 33, 37, 38, 39, 40, 53, 59, 86, 100, 108, 118, 124, 144
German Question, The, 22 n.
Germantown, 14 n.
Germany, 81, 106, 134
Gibbons, James Card., 24-26, 30, 32, 34, 35, 36, 38, 39, 44, 58, 60, 61, 67, 69, 72, 78, 79, 85, 87, 94

107, 108, 111, 112, 113, 115, 129 n., 138
Gigot, Francis E., 110
Gilmour, Bishop Richard, 37, 124
Gmeiner, Rev. John, 94
Gmunden, 46, 50
Goldach, 82, 83, 147, 148
Goldendale, Wis., 13
Gold standard, 74
Gonner, Mr. Nicholas, 118
Good Shepherd, House of, 79
Goral, Rev. B. E., 114
Gospels, The Four Examined, 16
Grace, Bishop Thomas L., 21, 24, 35, 47
Grand Rapids, 37, 38
Greenbacks, 74
Green Bay, 20, 22 n., 39, 48, 49, 61, 87, 88, 98, 122, 124
Green Bay Advocate, 55 n.
Green Bay State Gazette, 88, 89, 94
Gulski, Rev. Hyacinth, 72
Gymnasium at seminary, 121

Haas, Bishop Francis J., 113, 145
Handbook for Catholic Parishioners, 125, 145 n.
Hanna, Abp. Edward J., 110
Hannan, Rev., 55 n.
Harding, Warren G., 113
Hartford, 47, 71
Harvard University, 109
Havre, Le, 10
Hayes, Abp. Patrick, 139
Heath, Frederick, 141
Heckerism, 104
Hegel, George, 52, 53
Heiss, Mr. Joseph, 9
Heiss, Abp. Michael, 9-46, 48, 49, 50, 51, 56, 58
Hellstern, Rev. J. H., 81 n.
Hengell, Rev. Henry, 45 n., 109
Hennessy, Abp. John, 80
Henni, Abp. John M., 12 n., 13, 14, 17, 18, 20, 21, 22, 23, 26, 27, 28, 29, 39, 47, 83
Heresy, 78, 117
Hergenroether, Joseph Card., 27

Heuser, Rev. Herman J., 86
Highland, 42 n.
History, 111
Hoan, Mayor Daniel, 134-135, 141
Hoard, Gov. William D., 51, 53
Hodnett, Rev. Thomas P., 72
Hodur, Rev. Francis, 116
Hollanders, 59
Hollergschwandtner, Rev., 46, 50
Holy Days, 31 n.
Holy Ghost, 76, 123
Holy Land, 72
Holy Name Society, 146
Holy Trinity Church, Cincinnati, 13
Holzhauser, Rev. Bartholomew, 20, 21
Homesickness of Heiss, 17
Horstmann, Bishop Ignatius F., 66
Hotels preferred by Messmer, 147
Housekeepers, 20
Hubertus, 13
Huerta, Victoriano, 137
Hugenroth, Rev. B., 50
Hughes, Abp. John, 62
Hughes-Wilson campaign, 135
Humanitarianism of Socialists, 141, 142
Humanum Genus, 66
Hurter, Frederick E., 16
Hydrotherapy, 72

Immigrant and Land Bureau, 100
Immigration, 12, 36, 39, 40, 43, 60, 93, 100, 123, 144
Imprimatur, 16
Inama, Rev. Adalbert, 16
Incorporation, 29, 71 n., 80, 125
Index, Roman, 116
Indian missions, 23 n., 79
Indians, 59, 79
Indian schools, 79, 105, 106
Indifference, Religious, 34, 67, 69
Indulgences, 129
Industrial school, 29
Infallibility, papal, 22, 91
Ingolstadt, 14 n., 20
Innocent III, Life of, 16
Innsbruck, 31, 50, 83

Interdenominational meetings, 75
Interdict, 120
Inventories, 125
Ireland, Abp. John, 15 n., 22 n., 29, 32, 34, 36, 39, 41, 43, 44, 48, 49, 56, 57 n., 58, 64, 65, 67, 71 n., 73 n., 74, 78, 81, 86, 87, 89, 92, 105, 107, 108, 113, 138
Irish, 38, 41, 42 n., 55 n., 56, 118, 134, 136
Irish bishops, 38, 39
Iron Port, The, 55
Irvington, 85
Italy, 136

Jacquemin, Msgr. George, 107
Janesville, Gazette, 97
Jansenistic quibbling, 77
Japanese Martyrs, 83
Jefferson, Wis., 13, 16, 23
Jesuits, 23, 41, 46, 47, 48, 65, 104, 110
Jordan, Rev. Francis, 73
Josephism, 19, 62
Junior clergy examinations, 33

Kain, Abp. John J., 78
Kampf der Gegenwart, Der, 48, 67
Katholikentag, 126 n.
Katolik, 114
Katzer, Carl, 46
Katzer, Abp. Frederick, 32, 33 n., 43, 44, 46-82, 86, 88, 98, 107, 115, 119, 123, 145 n.
Keane, Abp. John J., 15 n., 22 n., 39, 85, 86, 87, 99, 104, 138
Kelley, Bishop Francis, 138
Kelly, Thomas, 55 n.
Kenrick, Abp. Francis P., 68
Kenrick, Abp. Peter R., 41
Kentucky, 10, 12
Keppeler, Rev. Francis A., 14
Kersten, Rev. Norbert, 80
Kleiner, Rev. Kilian, 19
Kneipp, Msgr. Sebastian, 72
Knights of Columbus, 136, 146
Knights of Labor, 34, 69
Knights of Pythias, 67, 68, 69

Know-nothing Party, 12 n., 17
Koudelka, Bishop Joseph M., 124
Kozlowski, Bishop Edward, 124
Krautbauer, Bishop Francis X., 28, 48, 49
Kruszka, Michael, 114
Kruszka, Rev. Wenceslaus, 115, 124
Kuhr, Rev. Ferdinand, 11, 12 n.
Kulturkampf, 62
Kundig, Rev. Martin, 25, 26, 110
Kuryer Polski, 114, 116, 117, 119

Labor unions, 34, 68, 72, 105, 106, 112, 126, 140
La Crosse, 20, 21, 22, 23, 27, 39, 59, 71, 87, 122
La Fayette, S. S., 22
La Follette, Robert M. Sr., 134
Laity, 114, 117, 119
La Pointe, 23 n.
Latin terminology, 84
Lawler, John, 36
Lawsuits, 81 n., 117
Ledochowski, Mieceslaus Card., 64
Lefevere, Bishop Peter Paul, 21
Lenroot, Senator Irvine, 113
Leo XIII, Pope, 34, 65, 66, 72, 75, 79, 80, 84, 91, 105, 115
Leo House, 40
Leopoldine Society, 11, 47, 50
Libel suit, 81 n.
Liberalism, 68, 75, 94-95, 97, 98, 108
Liberty bonds, 136
Libraries, 125-126
Lieber, Dr., 72
Liège, 50
Lincoln, Abraham, 17, 18
Linz, 50, 62, 72
Liquor, 41, 99, 140
Lithuanians, 121, 136
Liturgy, 31, 129
Louisville, 10, 11, 12, 12 n.
Louvain, 31
Loyalty
  During Mexican War, 17
  During World War, 134-137
Ludwig Mission Society, 10, 11, 11 n., 14, 50

INDEX

Lutherans, 44, 51, 57, 133
Luzern Conspiracy, 93. See also Cahensly

Maccabees, The, 69
Madero, Francis I., 137
Madison, 103
Madison Democrat, 55 n.
Manitowoc, 122
Manitowoc Pilot, 97
Marathon, 146
Marinette,
    Messmer's speech at, 102
    North Star, 57 n.
Markett, Rev. Francis, 111
Marquette,
    Diocese of, 122
    Statue of, 102
    University, 110
Marty, Bishop Martin, 27 n., 32, 33, 36, 58, 82 n., 87
Marxism.
    See Socialism
Mary, Blessed Virgin, 20
Marytown, 135 n.
Mass, Attacked by Prohibition, 139
Masses
    for Poor Souls, 127
    High and Low, 127
    on All Souls' Day, 127-128
Mathew, Rev. Theobald, 41
Matrimony, 16, 101, 126
Maximilian of Mexico, 18, 47 n.
McCloskey, John Card., 30
McEvoy, Msgr. Mathew, 113
McFaul, Bishop James, 104, 107
McGinnity, Rev. E. M., 73
McGlynn, Rev. Edward, 74 n.
McGrady, Rev. Thomas M., 101
McKinley, William, 74, 101
McMahon, Miss Ella, 110
McMaster, James, 31 n.
McQuaid, Bishop Bernard, 35, 82, 87, 109
Melcher, Bishop Joseph, 22
Memoirs of Heiss, 17
Memoriale sulla Questione dei Tedeschi, 37, 38, 41

Merrill, 123
Messmer, Joseph, 83
Messmer, Abp. Sebastian, 40, 49 n., 82-148
Messmer High School, 144
Method of Christian Doctrine, 110
Mexico,
    Trade with, 74
    Uprisings in, 137-138
    War with, 17
Meyer vs. Nebraska, 62 n.
Militia of Christ, 112
Milwaukee,
    City politics, 141
    Conference of Catholic Charities, 114
    Diocese of, 12, 24
    Provincial council of, 32, 49, 126
Milwaukee Journal, 139
Milwaukee Sentinel, 40, 51, 59, 94, 96, 97, 132
Missions, Parish, 13, 33
Mississippi River, 10
Mitre of Katzer, 49
Mixed marriage, 28
Modern Woodman, 69
Moehler, John A., 16
Moeller, Abp. Henry, 112
Monastic life, 76
Monroe Doctrine, 60, 134
Moore, Bishop John, 37
Morality, Socialist, 142-143
Most Holy Redeemer, Archbasilica of, 79
Motu Proprio of 1903, 129
Mt. Calvary, Wis., 84
Mt. Mary College, 23
Moynihan, Msgr. James H., 95 n.
Muehlsiepen, Rev. Henry, 39
Mueller, Rev. Joseph F., 17
Muench, Abp. Aloysius J., 113, 145
Muldoon, Bishop Peter J., 112, 125
Mundelein, Abp. George, 112 n.
Munich, 10, 14, 15 n., 16, 17, 72
Munich, University of, 16
Music, Church. See Church Music
Mutual aid societies, 37, 49, 106

Naples, 72, 148
Napoleon III, Emperor, 19
Nashville, 38
National Educational Association, 56
Nationalism, 12 n., 24, 26, 36, 58 n., 60, 80, 86, 117, 126
National parishes, 37
N. C. W. C., 113
Nebraska vs. Meyer, 62
Negroes, 12, 18, 141, 144
Neo-Manichaeism, 139
Neuberg, 9,
Newark, 84
New Orleans, 10
Newport, Ky., 12 n.
New World, The, 90
New York, 22, 72, 83, 84
New York, Provincial council of, 84
New York *World*, 73 n.
Niagara Falls Conference, 137
North Star, Marinette, 57 n.
Northwestern Chronicle, 81, 86, 95 n., 98
Notre Dame, School Sisters of, 23, 38 n., 48, 72
Notre Dame University, 28 n., 49, 103
Novalis, 41
Nowiny Polski, 114
Nursing, 73
Nymphenburg, 10

Obedience, 71
Oberlin, 109 n.
O'Connell, Bishop Denis, 39, 84, 87, 104, 107, 108
O'Connell, William Card., 139
Odd Fellows, 67, 68, 69, 70 n.
O'Gorman, Bishop Thomas, 103, 104 n.
O'Hearn, Rev. D. J., 44, 126
Ohio River, 10
Old Catholics, 88
Orange, N. J., 85
Orphans, 33 n., 89, 146
Oschwald, Rev. Ambrose, 73
Oshkosh, Wis., 55, 106, 121, 122

Oshkosh *Daily Northwestern*, 96
Outagamie County, 102
Overproduction, 74

Pabst residence, 147
Pace, Rev. E. A., 103
Pacifism, 134
Pallium
 of Heiss, 29
 of Henni, 24
 of Katzer, 60
 of Messmer, 107
Panic. See Depression
Parental rights, 43, 52, 56, 65, 94, 96, 97
Paris, 10
Parishes, Canonical rights of, 37
Parocchi, Lucido Card., 72
Parochial schools, 28, 29, 31, 37, 50, 62, 63-66, 71, 75, 80, 86, 89, 90, 91, 94, 95, 98, 114 n., 125, 127, 133-134, 137
Pastor, Ludwig von, 112
Pastoral-Blatt, 19, 36, 37
Patriotism, 43, 75, 88, 95
Paullhuber, Rev. F. X., 14
Peck, Gov. George W., 56 n., 57
Peter Damian, St., 17
Peter's Pence, 79
Pettit, Rev. P. F., 26
Pfaldorf, 9
Philippine Question, 106, 107
Philosophy, 17, 31
Picnics, 28, 144
Pierz, Rev. Francis X., 46, 47
Pinten, Bishop Joseph G., 125
Pio Nono College. See Catholic Normal School
Pius IX, Pope, 83
Pius X, Pope, 125, 126, 127, 129, 131 n.
Pledge, 99
Poles, 56 n., 59, 89, 105 n., 114-121, 123, 124, 134, 136
Polish bishops, 114, 115, 116-118
Polish newspapers, 114
Polish priests, 114, 115, 116, 117, 141

INDEX

Politics, Civil, 56 n., 57 n.
Politics, Ecclesiastical, 57, 108
Populists, 73, 74
Prairie du Chien, 23, 36
Praxis Synodalis, 84
Prayers for armies, 128, 137
Premonstratensians, 89
Preuss, Arthur, 66 n.
Priesterverein, 39
Priests, Support of, 29, 49, 79 n.
Prieth, Rev. Godfried, 84, 85
Private judgment, 136
Profits of industrialists, 136
Progressives, 143
Prohibition, 88, 139
Propaganda College, 11
Propaganda, Congregation of the, 25, 27, 37, 39, 60
Propagation of the Faith, Society of the, 11 n.
Public schools, 11, 13, 31, 55 n., 56, 67 n., 75, 91, 95-98, 102, 114 n., 137, 141, 142
Purcell, Bishop John B., 10, 24
Purgatorial Society, 128
Purgatory, 127-128

Quod Apostolici Muneris, 105

Racial tension. See Nationalism.
Racial theories, 76
Railroads, 24
Rainer, Msgr. Joseph, 32 n., 80, 122, 135
Rampolla, Mariano Card., 72
Red Cross, 135, 137
Redeemer, Most Holy, Archbasilica of, 79
Reedy's Mirror, 66
Reisach, Charles Card., 10, 11, 35
Relatio de Questione Germanica, 15 n., 38, 39
Relief Committee, 112
Religious orders, 107
Republican Party, 55, 56, 60
Rerum Novarum, 34, 75, 106, 112
Residence of Milwaukee archbishops, 41, 71, 147

Retreats, 10, 19
Review (Preuss), 66 n.
Rhode, Bishop Paul P., 116, 124
Richter, Bishop Henry J., 37, 57, 58, 124
"Rietli," The, 83, 147
Rights of Child, 53, 130
Rights, Natural, 51-55
Rights, Parental, 43, 52, 56, 65, 94, 96, 97
Riordan, Abp. Patrick W., 78
Romana, 21 n.
Roman Question, 73 n., 136
Romanticism, German, 16
Rome, 11, 21, 22, 25, 30, 31, 32, 37, 41, 43, 49, 50, 58, 64, 65, 68, 69, 72, 73, 79, 83, 85, 104, 108, 115, 148
Roncetti, Msgr. Cesare, 23
Rorschah, 82
Rose, Mayor David, 141
Rotterdam, 72
Rouen, 10
Roxbury, 16
Rubrics, 129, 147
Rudigier, Bishop Francis J., 46, 47, 62
Ruegg, Bishop Ferdinand, 125
Rural life, 100

Sacred Heart College, 23
Sacred vessels, 28
St. Adalbert Church, Milw., 120
St. Aemilian's Orphanage, 15, 148
St. Agnes Hospital, Fond du Lac, 80
St. Albertus Magnus Verein, 48
St. Aloysius Institute, 89
St. Benedict the Moor Church, Milw., 144
St. Bernard's Home for Workingmen, 145
St. Bernard's Seminary, 35
St. Casimir Church, Milw., 120
St. Charles Home, Milw., 145
St. Charles Seminary, Phila., 86
St. Cloud, Minn., 24, 82 n., 87
St. Cyril and Methodius Church,

Milw., 120
St. Francis of Assisi Convent, 14, 15, 16, 23, 50
St. Francis Seminary, 19, 26, 29, 35, 41, 44, 47, 81, 82 n., 87, 88, 111, 121-122
St. Francis Xavier Cathedral, Green Bay, 48, 50
St. George Church, Milw., 119, 121
St. George College, 82
St. John's Abbey, Collegeville, 32
St. John's Cathedral, Milw., 29-30, 80, 135, 147
St. John's School for the deaf, 146
St. Josaphat's Church, Milwaukee, 116, 119
St. Joseph's Cathedral, La Crosse, 22
St. Joseph's Church, De Pere, 98
St. Leo Benevolent Society, 49
St. Leo's Church, Irvington, 85
St. Louis, Mo., 19, 24, 32, 37, 38, 39, 41
St. Louis Church, Munich, 49
St. Margaret's Guild, 145
St. Mary Czestochowa Church, 120
St. Mary Major, 82 n.
St. Mary's Church, La Crosse, 22
St. Mary's Church, Milwaukee, 13, 14 n., 15 n., 16
St. Michael's Priest Fund, 79 n., 128
St. Monica Church, Whitefish Bay, 113
St. Nazianz, Wis., 73
St. Norbert's College, 89
St. Patrick's Church, Fort Howard, 88
St. Paul, Minn., 32, 47
St. Paul's Chapel, Madison, 110
St. Peter Damian, Life of, 17
St. Peter and St. Paul Church, Milw., 124
St. Peter's Church, Newark, 84, 87
St. Raphael's Society, 36, 93, 99
St. Rose Convent, La Crosse, 44
St. Stanislaus Church, Milw., 124
St. Sulpice, Paris, 10

St. Venantius Church, Orange, 85
St. Vincent de Paul Society, 145
Salary of clergy, 33, 125
Salesianum, 110
Saloons, 42, 97, 126, 139
Salvatorians. See Divine Savior.
Salzmann, Rev. Joseph, 15, 16, 18, 19, 38 n., 45, 47, 48
Satolli, Abp. Francis, 65, 89, 90, 91, 98
Schinner, Bishop Augustine F., 123-124
Schism, 88-89, 115, 116
Schonat, Rev. William, 10
School, Industrial, 29
School board, Milwaukee, 141
School money, 133 n.
Schools. See Parochial Schools, Public Schools.
Schrembs, Bishop Joseph, 138 n.
Schroeder, Rev. Joseph, 66, 108
Schwarzenbruner, Barbara, 46
Schwebach, Bishop James, 71, 80
Scruples of Katzer, 63 n.
Secular colleges, Catholics at, 109
Secularism, 62
Seebote, Der, 18
Seidel, Mayor Emil, 141
Seidenbusch, Bishop Rupert, 24, 28, 32, 48
Self determination, 134
Seminaries, Education in, 31, 32 n., 35
Seton Hall, 82, 85, 87, 104, 110
Sevastopol, Wis., 89
Shawano County Journal, 57 n.
Shea, John Gilmary, 36, 37
Sheboygan, 106
Sherman, Rev. Thomas F., 141
Sick, Nursing of, 73
Silver, Free coinage of, 74
Simeoni, John Card., 26, 32 n., 39
Singenberger, Sir John B., 19, 31, 87, 129, 147
Sisters teaching in public schools, 102
Siupecki, Congressman, 56 n.
Slavery, 12, 17

Smedding, Rev. Benedict, 21 n.
Smith-Towner Bill, 133
Social Democratic Party, 74, 140
Socialism and Socialists, 34, 73, 74, 97, 105, 106, 126, 132-133, 140-143
Social problems, 73, 74, 75, 105, 112-113
Societies, Catholic, 123, 133, 140, 145. See also Federation of Catholic Societies.
Societies, Secret, 34, 66-70, 75, 145 n.
Soldiers, 128, 137
Sons of Temperance, 68, 69
South America, 74
Spain, 127
Spain, War with, 75, 105, 107
Spalding, Bishop John L., 25-26, 34, 35, 36, 58, 61, 105 n.
Spalding, Abp. Martin J., 12 n., 20
Spirago, Francis, 110
Sports, 127
Spring Bank, Wis., 113
State, Rights of, 43, 51-54, 64, 66, 72, 97, 101, 133
State Gazette. See Green Bay *State Gazette.*
Statistics, 21, 23, 38, 40, 50, 59, 63, 86, 88, 124, 144 n.
Stehling, Rev. Edward, 135 n.
Steiger, Rev. Mathias, 14
Steinhuber, Andrew Card., 72
Stevens Point, 117, 123
Strasbourg, 10
Strele, Rev., 47
Stritch, Abp. Samuel, 118
Sturgeon Bay, Wis., 89
Sunday rest, 42
Superior, Diocese of, 121, 122, 124
Suspension, 118, 120
Sweeting, Assemblyman, 102
Symbolik, 16
Synods, 23, 29, 32 n., 50, 71, 79 n., 126
Szukalski, Rev., 121

Taverns. See saloons.

Teachers, Public school, 56, 98
Temperance, 99, 139
Temporal power of pope. See Roman Question.
Textbooks
  Free, 132-133, 141
  Standard, 80
Thanksgiving Day, 142
Theology Courses, 31
"Thy Kingdom Come", 112
Tolerari Potest, 64, 65
Total Abstinence, 41, 42, 99
Trade, 74
Traudt, Rev. Bernard G., 134, 147
Traunsee, 49
Trustees, 125
Truth Teller, The, 42 n.
Turnverein, 43
Two Rivers Chronicle, 98

Ulrich, Rev. Constantine, 89
Utrecht, Schismatic Church of, 116

Vanguard, The, 102 n.
Van Hise, Charles, 108
Varela, Rev. Felix, 42 n.
Vatican Council, 22
Veendam, S. S., 72
Vertin, Bishop John, 32, 49
Vestments, 28
Vicar generals, 39
Vilatte, "Abp." Joseph R., 88-89, 115
Villas for seminarians, 31
Vincennes, Ind., 37
Vocations, 31
Volstead law, 140

Wages, 74
Wahrheitsfreund, Der, 19
Waloon Belgian Catholics, 59
Wapelhorst, Rev. Christopher, 20 n., 31
Ward Co., The, 121-122
Ward, Rev. Mathias J., 42
Watertown, 132
Wausau, 123
Weber, Abp. Joseph, 124

Wigger, Bishop Winand M., 58 n., 87
Willard, Rev. George L., 26, 42
William II, Emperor, 134
Wilson, Woodrow, 134, 137, 138
Winnebago, Lake, 84
Wisconsin Catholic Publishing Co., 118
Wisconsin Country Life Conference, 100
Wisconsin Historical Society, 111
Wisconsin Rapids, 123
Wisconsin Supreme Court, 81 n., 118
Wisconsin, University of, 108, 109
Wisconsin Vorwaerts, 140
Woerishofen, 72

Woman
  and socialism, 141
  extravagence of, 132
  in choirs, 129
  suffrage, 132, 142
Wood, Abp. James F., 30
World, The New York, 73 n.
World War I, 66, 112, 113, 128, 134-137, 144
Wuerzburg, 15 n.

Zahm, Rev. John A., 103, 104
Zardetti, Bishop Otto, 72, 82, 83, 87
Zeininger, Msgr. August, 48, 50, 65, 72, 73 n., 74
Zuber, Bishop Athanasius, 83

RET'D SEP 28 1987